The Art of Fine Gardening

The Art of Fine Gardening

CRAIG BERGMANN LANDSCAPE DESIGN

Craig Bergmann with Russell Buvala

Foreword by Roy Diblik

M

Contents

Foreword

Roy Diblik

We all share one activity each day, no matter who we are, where we are, or what undertakings we have on hand: we start that new day by going outside. That moment we step outdoors and leave our home, our shelter, we instantly become immersed in our surroundings. All our focused thoughts and diverse actions are enhanced and driven by our five senses, along with our human inner awareness of health, beauty, and love.

How do we live within our own nature? How does nature appear to us? And what makes something healthy and beautiful? These questions give rise to thoughts that frame our way of being and connect us to all our future possibilities. We are totally immersed in place wherever we are, whether that's a neighborhood space, a parking lot, a public park large or small, a commercial area, or a shopping district. These are all planted places. Too often they're planted with unimaginative and unquestioned low-common-denominator landscape practices that have no identity, no emotion, and no relationship to people and place. As we grew up with these landscapes, however, we believed them to be beautiful.

In the 1970s and 1980s accumulating conversations began taking place about perennial plants, native plants, plant composition, and planting design. As our thoughts and awareness of plants expanded, so did our planting practices. People began to experience and discover that diverse perennial and native plantings made them feel "better." This movement had many creative contributors, and Craig Bergmann was one of its earliest influences. He is skillful at coordinating styles, gathering artistic emotions, and constantly discovering what makes a place beautiful. Early on in his career, Craig met and hired Russ Buvala. Russ was able to interpret the emotions Craig wanted to impart, and to translate that into practical ways to care for and enhance Craig's garden designs.

It's their long collaboration that sets their plantings apart from other current garden design. Their gardens have workability. Their deep horticultural knowledge allows them to give thoughtful attention to plant placement, creating plant communities that live well, can be enhanced, and can be cared for with smart gardening practices. Not only have they inspired plant-driven garden design, they have also developed a solid way of caring for plants as a group. Craig realized that the old saying "right plant, right place" was missing one component. The phrase should be "right plant, right place, right plant relationships." When young plants can grow into each other in harmony, the garden is off to a good beginning.

I've known Craig since 1981. I was managing a perennial plant nursery then, The Natural Garden. We grew about 175 various perennials and native plants, all in the ground. I would walk up and down the paths between them with the customers, helping them to choose plants. I would dig up those they liked and charge them fifty cents a plant. Craig would come out after visiting other nurseries in the area, walk up and down the paths, and ask questions about almost every plant. I always dug up at least a few plants for him at each visit. He would quickly come to know them, what their personalities are, and how they like to live. As his awareness of perennials expanded, he began adding more and more diversity to his garden designs. It's clear that Craig's passion, persistence, curiosity, and his strong self-expressive nature guide his garden design and gardening experiences. Craig eventually decided to create a wonderful retail nursery of his own, combining traditional and contemporary garden plants; it influenced many of the gardeners and garden designers in the Midwest.

I met Russ and got to know him in 1991, as I was starting Northwind Perennial Farm with Colleen Garrigan and Steve Coster, my two partners, but I needed a day job until we could grow enough plants and generate enough project work to sustain the three of us. Craig invited me to work for a while with his garden care crew, headed up by Russ. For me it was a great adventure to shift from being a perennial and native plant grower to a practicing gardener. I came to know the plants I grew as partners in solid plant relationships.

From garden to garden, I recognized all the plants I had grown, now living in healthy plant communities. I have to say, it was very exciting and enlightening. My conversations with Craig and Russ along with the hands-on garden experiences were the beginning moments of finding my own way into perennial gardening.

For Craig and Russ, gardening is a real joy. That comes through in this book. They share deep plant knowledge as well as affection for all plants. As social media dominates our visual world and emphasizes impermanent snapshots of glamour, this book gives you the luxury of opening yourself up to the discovery of what whole, healthy, beautiful gardens look like. Take your time reading through their thoughts and observing their years of work. You may discover that soon in your own future you'll be asking yourself this question: what kind of meaningful garden space do I want to create? And you'll have fun doing it!

Introduction

While it's always on our mind, we know perfection when working with Mother Nature is never obtainable. Why, then, do we garden? It's the challenge and the reward a garden gives. A spectacular show of bloom or growth, a combination never before tried that reveals itself to be successful, having something happen that wasn't planned but is serendipitous—these moments give deep satisfaction to every gardener, and especially to us. Appreciating even fleeting moments of beauty make it all worthwhile. It has been proven that we have learned far more from our mistakes than our successes in our gardening efforts, and this hard-earned education informs our future pursuits for the better.

The most important lesson: don't overdo a good thing. Stop when the garden is on the edge of "perfect." Slight imperfections can make magic moments—cherish that. Pushing on can easily wind up looking too much like obvious human intervention. We have learned to enjoy the pursuit of attempting to manage plants. We ask Nature to accept our efforts, and in turn we try to honor and consider hers whenever we look to "improve" on something she is doing. In Greek mythology, Sisyphus was dealt the eternal punishment of rolling a boulder up a hill only to have it roll back down at the moment it was about to reach the top—fighting against Nature can feel like that. It's best to have a sense of humility when dealing with the reign of Mother Nature. This too enables our true collaborative work, together with nature to shine.

Our Wilmette garden: an intimate seating area (left) and the terrace with Rosie, a Tibetan terrier, presiding.

Past and present views to the West Gardens at the Gardens at 900.

Transforming any green space into an artful garden requires collaboration and expertise, a focus on craftsmanship, and long-term horticultural care. People often think that a garden designer's job ends once the plants are in the ground, but it's just as plantings begin to establish themselves that the most intense lens of observation is required on the part of both the owners, the gardeners, and the designers. Our Garden Care team is on the front line of this transition time from what starts as a group of plants and ultimately becomes a beautiful garden space. We can't say the day after installation that any of our gardens can be considered living art. We can tell you that it's only once our efforts are rooted in over one year, two, even three, and only after a few inevitable intentional tweaks—and accommodating the nuance of the unintended volunteer plants who join in along the way—that the essence of the garden will reveal itself in an exponential leap of beauty.

For nearly forty years, our firm has conceived, built, and reimagined many projects within the dynamic world of plants and gardening. We have always challenged each other and enjoyed the journey together. It's when we're given a prickly creative problem to address that our problem-solving receptors fire up and we enjoy ourselves the most. All this history has generated trust and a common garden language, one that we work to share with our staff of many talents. Our projects only come to life due to the exhaustive efforts of landscape architects, designers, growers, project managers, installers, gardeners, and horticulturalists. Their energy and their willingness to work collaboratively with clients, craftsmen, existing architecture, and with specialty plants and materials keeps our gardens feeling fresh and current.

What drove us into this profession and keeps us entranced by it after all this time? I think my passion for nature and ultimately gardening must have been influenced by my Native American heritage, from my mother's side of the family. On my fifth birthday, my father donated a 20-by-20-foot plot of ground behind the garage to me, as my very own garden space—I continued to play with it all the way through college, until my parents sold the house. This semi-shaded area had good native soil and was delineated from the rest of the yard by a low stone wall my dad built. When they replaced our old brick patio, I repurposed the bricks in my garden: the upcycling gardener was born! Fast forward five-plus years to when our local village lake, Lake Ellyn, was being dredged to remove a century's worth of silt. The lake water was pushed through a storm drain system that exited into a drainage canal across the street from our house—and the lake's population of foot-long goldfish (mostly dead) became an abundant source of what every American Indian could recognize as free fertilizer. Over many days, my best friend Duncan and I filled burlap sacks with them, pedaled them home on our bikes, and planted them among my crops. Our tomato harvests were insane that year—my dad had to string guide wires up the garage roof, the vines grew so high. We had to climb ladders to harvest the August bounty. Our dahlias were the size of platters, not dinner plates. My mom just shook her head, proud of her gardening boys. This explosive growth pleased me, because from the start I wanted my garden to look like it was established, like the beautiful mature woods across the street.

Dad and I would also take seasonal sojourns to our favorite nurseries and gardens. The Natural Garden was one of our favorites because we could talk about our passion for all plants with Craig Sensor, the owner, and Roy Diblik, who obviously left a lasting impression. These passions helped drive me toward later education in botany and biology and defined many of my life choices. Nature has always been, and remains, my guiding light in so many ways.

I have been blessed to share my adult life with two kindred spirits, and both have nurtured me and my career. In 1980 I met James Grigsby, a professor at the Art Institute of Chicago. Although as a family my parents would take us on rainy Sunday afternoons to the museums in Chicago (my favorite picks were the Art Institute, the Field Museum, and the Shedd Aquarium), I hadn't followed fine art as much as an adult. James encouraged me to gobble up everything from performance art in New York City to art installations in public parks. Our first Christmas together, James took me to a staff party at the president of the Art Institute's apartment. I had never seen truly great fine art hanging outside of a museum until then, and I was wowed that anyone would dare to hang a Monet over an aquarium. James became my life and business partner, cofounding and supporting CBLD in every way. Sadly, in 2002 we lost him from complications a month after successful brain tumor surgery, but I still thank him and work hard to honor his trust in me.

Years passed, and I felt sufficiently happy in my own skin. James and I had had more than twenty wonderful years together. Many never find love like that, so I never expected another relationship of equal seriousness. Then, on a hot July afternoon at a lakeside commitment

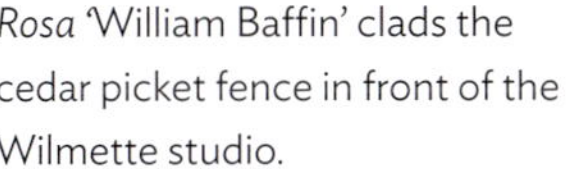

Rosa 'William Baffin' clads the cedar picket fence in front of the Wilmette studio.

ceremony of some friends, I met Paul Klug. Since 2005, Paul has been my home, my love, and my spouse. As we grow older, we both realize that we are partly who we are because, like neighboring trees in a forest, our roots are entwined, and we grow stronger together than we ever could alone.

An energetic young boy, Russell Buvala, now CBLD's head gardener, was also introduced to gardening by his parents. His house was set on an acre of land, and for many years the back third would be deeply disced open by a farmer for his dad to plant with vegetables. He "worked" alongside him at sowing time . . . mostly playing in the dirt. When left to their own devices, he and his brother Randy would build forts out of the dried clay clods, each lobbying chunks at the other's stronghold. Simply amazing fun with plain old dirt.

A raised bed immediately adjacent to the house was earmarked for his mother's rose garden. His father filled the raised beds with a rich, sandy, humus-like soil, and with that soil came weed seeds galore. His job was to help his mom clear the garden of the "invaders." The soil was so loose he remembers simply being able to run his hands just under the surface, like a living scuffle hoe, to uproot them. It was gloriously satisfying to him to be able to clean it so easily and completely. Throughout the yard were old apple and a few peach trees that provided some great climbing—and eating! Being in such a diverse environment where he could build forts to play in, play in leftover sandpiles from building materials, climb trees, watch ants make massive mounds, and see how all the mostly unkept lawn and insect life interacted allowed Russell to be analytical of what nature was teaching. Gardening was planted in him at an early age.

Our Early History

The decision to start a gardening company started back in 1980 when I was working part-time at a downtown Chicago flower shop called Bunches, around school hours at DePaul University where I was studying biology and botany. A very nice woman, Mrs. Ryan, came into the shop

Perspective sketch of an early landscape project.

900 studio design chat with omnipresent resident Norwich terriers.

and asked me who had arranged the buckets of flowers on the sidewalk and made up the bouquets so nicely. That job fell to whichever employee opened the shop on any given day—in this case, me. She and her husband hired me soon thereafter, becoming my first design and installation job. I, and later CBLD, maintained the property for more than thirty years, until Mr. Ryan passed and Mrs. Ryan downsized into a condominium.

Mrs. Ryan gave me and my skills as a gift (in her eyes) to her husband for his fiftieth birthday, at first to help him with his perennial garden. It surrounded the beautiful brick patio behind their formal Benjamin Marshall–designed house in Kenilworth, Illinois, an affluent suburb I was unfamiliar with until my first visit to their property. "Not a bad place to start the business!" said James, when he heard of my first commission. He told me that he would help manage the financial part of the job if I managed the plant and art part. Craig Bergmann Landscape Design, Inc., was born. Our initial office was in our second-story city apartment. We shared a VW Rabbit pickup truck we called "Tonka" and had access to a stockpile of topsoil from a friend, Gunnar Piotter, who had an established landscape company in the city.

Once we had the Ryans' project under our belt and a few referrals from James's friends in the art world, we needed staff to help us build our gardens and to find a suburban home for our company. A dear artist friend, Lee Schillereff, in Wilmette was so excited by our success that she suggested we buy her house (just three blocks from the Ryans) because it included a

Russell Buvala in the garden.

greenhouse, a studio building, and a massive garage. We were in business on the North Shore. In a wonderful bit of serendipity, it emerged that Lee was great friends with Sylvia Shaw Judson, granddaughter of Howard Van Doren Shaw, the architect whose residential projects from the early 1900s have become many of our favorite project sites in Lake Forest; a few are featured in this book.

Our first full-time employee was Christel Radloff, a recent graduate of the Art Institute of Chicago, where James ran the Young Artists Studio. Her artistically trained eye translated almost immediately to garden care. A ravenous reader and a quick study, Christel excelled, and her enthusiastic personality resonated well with clients and fellow employees. When a local perennial plant nursery decided to close their nearby suburban location not long after that, we were happy to hire some of their employees. Jose Ochoa came on first. We built a crew of three men to help me install designs that I was drawing after hours and on the weekends. We were growing rapidly and needed some serious horticulturalists. I asked Dianne Noland, a teacher at the horticulture school at the University of Illinois Urbana-Champaign, and she recommended two of her star students: Russell Buvala and Deanna Carlson. Russ was in his last year and was the flower show chairman for the horticulture club, and Deanna was just graduating with great plant ID skills, plant knowledge, and innate growing talent. Russ joined just after graduation in February of 1988. Deanna followed in August as our first perennial grower and propagator at our eventual nursery location in Winthrop Harbor, Illinois. Jane Johnson soon came on as our senior grower of seasonal flowers at the nursery, where she still presides over our twenty-plus greenhouses and growing staff. Jane and Deanna continued to grow for decades until we lost Deanna, Russell's wife, in 2023. The Buvala family has been present and essential throughout the growth of the company we have all created.

Now we had the makings of a real workplace, staffed with knowledgeable and dedicated people, great clients that trusted us from the beginning, and gobs of enthusiasm for what was ahead. The decision to begin installing true, full gardens of both herbaceous and woody plantings begged the question of who could/should maintain them long-term. We did not want to get into turf care or snowplowing, but still wanted to help our gardens thrive. Gardening in our area at the time was quite a specialty service; this work was mostly performed on the larger estates by private gardeners or the homeowners themselves. Our garden care department was born, with Russell at the helm, and he is still there today.

After installing projects for three years, our company grew and so did our Garden Care Department. With Roberto Hernanadez and ultimately Alfonso Hernandez joining Russell and Jose, we had an incredible, practical team of knowledgeable gardeners that is still the core of our workforce today. This group filled the bill with knowledge, intelligence, charm, malleability, and physical and mental toughness. Jose retired two years ago; the rest still work at CBLD. Alfonso's wife, Esmeralda, came on board soon after his arrival (over twenty-five years ago) as our first office staff member—she is still with us today.

Designing on the fly and on weekends was a daunting and impossible way to keep going and growing, so we hired a wonderful roster of designers and landscape architects over the early years at our Wilmette-based studio including Cathy Dammann, John Ciecielski, Charles Fischer, and Donald Bolak. These dedicated and talented professionals kept upping our design game and presence in the garden-making world. Donald made the move with us to Lake Forest and has been contributing his talents to CBLD for twenty-seven years now! Some of Don's projects are included here, along with some of his beautiful photography—another of his passions.

Now more than one hundred staff members strong, it is fascinating to me to tally that twenty-six folks have with the company over ten years, and eleven have been with us for over twenty-five years. And we still maintain that first full property design and installation project from 1985! Our staff and clients stick with us more often than not, and by this I am quite humbled.

The Country Garden

After years of renting farmland to grow uncommon and larger plants we needed, in 1988 we purchased a 22-acre parcel in Winthrop Harbor, Illinois, and called it The Country Garden. This affordable piece of land, abutting a landfill, allowed us room to grow into a space we had not yet completely defined. We could finally have container-grown nursery stock materials stored and available for year-round use. Before then, we had been storing plants on our driveway and growing plants on the garage roof in Wilmette, where James and I lived and worked. In 1989 we decided to open a garden center on the nursery property for the public, to help expand our plant offerings in the northern Illinois area.

The Country Garden retail lot in full summer bloom.

James and Craig are engulfed by the seasonal glory of the Autumn Garden.

Special events are an opportunity to share our talents at a smaller scale. An autumnal tower welcomes harvest dinner guests into the event; Detail of a show garden featuring a strap-metal sphere with its color orchestrated with old morel-like terra-cotta edging and *Helleborus* 'Ivory Prince'.

We created and installed display gardens on themes of sun and shade perennials, roses, herbs, aquatic and edible plantings. "The Autumn Garden," a very popular and national award-winning garden scheme, was completely devoted to celebrating the glories of that season, unusual for the era.

We were open to the public for sixteen years, with many dedicated customers making seasonal sojourns to the place. Jose Ochoa was the proud lead gardener of the display gardens under Russ's and my supervision for twelve years. The gardens were like his children, and he was so happy to share his knowledge with visitors.

We strove to always offer old and new varieties of hardy plants that were difficult to find in our general vicinity. People weren't usually seeking out native plants back then per se, so we would often buy them bare root from sustainable growers and only offer them in our spring season. Jane and Deanna, our growers, were incredibly busy cultivating more fantastic plants, of all sorts from woodies to herbaceous, seasonal annuals to nonhardy plants in unique forms and sizes. I miss the artful aspect of this growing concern we all created together.

Part of our firm's identity is wrapped up in the special events we have created for the public to experience, and having more space to grow what we needed for show gardens and one-off displays has also allowed us to participate in them. When I elected to exhibit in the first Chicago Flower and Garden Show in March 1995, Deanna, Jane, and Russell forced plants into flowering early for staging. All our show gardens acknowledge the reality of weeds, so they forced dandelions too—realistic details make the difference in helping people relate show gardens to home gardens and prove that we don't take ourselves too seriously. Since then, we've been involved in staging garden displays for many events at the Chicago Flower and Garden Show, the Chicago Botanic Garden, art openings, client weddings, and antiques shows, among others.

I will say, though, that I was once asked if the garden center and gardens was my hobby or part of the business. We never made enough money for all the effort it took to present the place to our standards—we offered more than seven hundred herbaceous plant varieties each summer season! After persistently being asked to sell the lot to the landfill company,

Successfully transplanted from the Country Garden, the *Gleditsia triacanthos var. inermis* 'Sunburst' is now the centerpiece of the motor court at 900.

we made the decision to let them have it in 2010; the profit allowed for the creation of a new, more focused, distribution-driven nursery facility and a new home for the design studio.

Jose redirected his attention to the Gardens at 900, our new company headquarters and my home; we relocated many of the plants in the various display gardens here. Purchasing and building the Gardens at 900 also provided Paul and me with a collective purpose—to save the great site and breathe new life into a space that was destined for the wrecking ball.

Years before, we had built a pavilion honoring James on The Country Garden site. This structure and the surrounding gardens celebrated James's passion for the quirky, folklike qualities in creative buildings and gardens. His passion for cooking, his love of blue flowers, and his attraction to brilliant chartreuse foliage were all incorporated into this project. We used the glorified park structure for outdoor activities, workshops, and to provide a shaded meeting or lunch area for visiting garden clubs. All the elements of this building and gardens were repurposed and given away when we sold, to keep James's memory alive and contributing somewhere. His 'Sunburst' honey locust now overlooks the center of the Motor Court at the Gardens at 900, for example. This chartreuse-leafed tree was incorporated into my wedding ceremony to Paul in 2014, as a massive chandelier holding of hundreds of votive candles under the reception tent. We loved that James could in this way be part of such a big day in our lives. Still today, we hear people say they miss The Country Garden but have plants from there thriving in their own gardens, and just as we were glad to be able to share pieces of James's memorial with people who are important to us, we think it's the highest compliment that our plants have endured to provide our clients and customers and friends enjoyment, year after year.

Our Process

My own process is anything but standardized. I am a very visual person, and would say that once I've visited a site, I will retain an almost photographic memory of it. When I first "meet" a property, I prefer to walk around it by myself, do a drive by, and look at real estate pictures (if available) just to distill what seems most interesting—often before meeting the owners. A new project will run its own show in my head for a while. This helps me immensely when I am scheming while daydreaming, long before I ever put pen to paper to articulate a design to others through sketches or in studio meetings.

Without these various visual ways of approaching a project, I couldn't do my best work. Truly getting to know a site from top to bottom before attempting to change it is my goal. My gut reaction to spaces, people, and plants has always been my design compass.

Translating vague ideas into a set of construction documents for others to follow is a whole other can of worms—thank God for my staff. They are much more technically trained than I am, which lets me focus on the big picture while we can still be precise as an office. They make each project not only possible to build, but also richer in beauty, detail, and environmental consciousness. Our meetings about what a site needs after I share an initial impression are considered akin to a "safe space" in therapy, where all ideas are welcome to fully explore the project's potential.

I try to link the architecture to the site, of course. The site to the desired aesthetic. The aesthetic to the environment. As we design, my experience of what plant possibilities are for the spaces and what they need to thrive becomes my secret weapon, as it were. As any home gardener knows, attempting to grow a plant provides much more information about what makes it happy than you can learn from a book or a website. Having designed and gardened for myself and others for decades now, this roster of hundreds of projects have served, essentially, as lab experiments where we have introduced many hypotheses—some proved, many disproved. Maintaining the sites we design long after installation compounds our connection to the project and provides invaluable opportunities to add to our expertise.

Old white oaks were carefully preserved during construction of a new house. Garden walls were suspended on steel grade beams between concrete piers to avoid damaging the roots.

Paving details can put the art in fine gardening. This sinuous path of reclaimed terra-cotta roofing tiles emulates the English Arts and Crafts style, while "crazy paving" of collected materials animates a cottage garden.

There are many more landscape professionals available for homeowners to hire today than when we started in the 1980s. One fact that distinguishes CBLD and has enabled us to endure all these decades is that we take the time to explore a site's possibilities and look at land as a piece of dynamic art, not just "a home landscape." We provide a palette of ideas, if you will, and with our clients, collectively choose from those options to create a truly personalized space that has a foundation of permanence with an artistic and horticulturally driven result. This takes time to create, and we take this time up front to do our best work. James once said to a potential client who asked why we charge for our designs, "We do not discount our talent. Building materials are for discounting." The creative and artistic expression of the final project is dependent on this process-journey. We also install 98 percent of our local work. This allows us to control the interpretation of the design against reality and select all materials needed to achieve the best result for the client.

I have always remembered a bumper sticker that read: "Be green, buy antiques." This represents how I approach a project from inception. Whether it is honoring the existing or bringing in new materials, I always try to use reclaimed materials from as many sources as possible to bring an established, aged finish to a project. Plants with an old character help visually settle a new planting. Often, the scale of an old plant is the only thing that will look proportionately correct in front of the architecture.

Similarly, old or repurposed materials and objects used in an ornamental way (as hardscape, for example) gives a new garden an immediate backstory. Age always makes people think as they experience a garden, whether they realize it or not; antique or reused materials make it feel like a place, not just a fleeting or seasonal sensory experience. New isn't necessarily better, it is just different from old.

If a project has historic architecture or a preexisting garden, we will search available archives to understand what had been there before to see if any old remnants can be featured, found, preserved, or reimagined for today. Working on historic sites is exciting to me; I have always looked at projects with the view of keeping worthy elements. I often hear at a final project walkthrough with clients that they feel "it looks like it has been there for years." That is the best compliment. For me it means that they are happy, that they feel settled in their established neighborhood, and that the long journey is over, and they can get on with living in their garden every day.

Similarly, keeping large plants in a newly conceived layout can make a project. I have asked clients to shrink the footprint of a new house to save a two-hundred-year-old oak more than once. A few times, they have listened. Saving such plants is a challenge when so much change is about to occur around them. We have all heard that the older one is, the more challenging change can be; imagine you're the tree and the appealing environment you have helped create over decades or even centuries is about to change drastically, but you're unable to move out of the way! If we as professionals advocating for the natural world do not represent a tree's best interest, who will? When it comes to trying to save old trees, we always consult trusted arborists to determine if the tree could survive the impact of the project and if there is anything we could do before, during, or post construction to aid in its chances of survival. Preconstruction meetings always include arborists' thoughts before any regrading or digging. If we are being hired to speak plant, then we must speak for both the existing and the new plant community—and for neighboring plantings as well, since plants famously do not respect arbitrary property boundaries.

It's also critical for us to communicate to everyone involved in a new project that it can be necessary to refine a design along the way. Projects that have been interrupted, stopped and started, or led by outside contributors before being turned over to us can involve hard-to-rectify results that were decided on the fly or on paper only, without vetting the impact on the final project. We keep our eyes and ears open to all the goings-on of a project as it evolves, and tweaking along the way as necessary. This is essential for achieving a satisfying result. As landscape experts, we must follow arboriculture and horticulture requirements on our projects. Existing soil conditions can often be learned by studying the quality and condition of the plantings already growing on the site. Weeds and old trees will tell us all a lot if we just listen to them. Sometimes we will have to walk away from a project if we feel the worthy plant elements would be too abused or unacknowledged as important, if they are clearly considered secondary to the construction.

We often specify terraces and hardscape elements in our designs; that's the easy part. Installing and nurturing softscape is the hardest part of any garden. Using the wrong base material on a patio or planter can permanently change the soil pH and, in essence, poison the soil for some plants. The hardscape does not pay the price, the plants do—and ultimately, the client. And we also try to consider municipal infrastructure beyond our control. In one case, underground water lines improperly flowed into our project's legal surface drainage sewer connection. The result was a two-foot-high by eighteen-inch-wide geyser spewing out of a manhole cover and flooding a brand-new landscape during every above-average rain event. Supposedly, all the right checks were in place, but one solution caused another problem. Although checking underlying structures hardly provides the gratification of setting out plants, it's critical to do our homework.

After a newly installed landscape has settled in, there is a time of hypergrowth from the plants and excitement on the part of the owners about the impact the landscape is providing. During this active time, our Garden Care team begins to build its long-term relationship with both the client and the garden. Our short Midwestern growing season puts a lot of

View from the bridge over the old water garden allows for a broader perspective.

demands on gardeners trying to control the chaos week by week and year over year during these intense, seasonal bursts. We have developed preplanned logistical processes and "tricks of the trade" to help counteract the tornadic effects of having to plant seasonal containers, needing to stake plants that seem to grow exponentially right before your eyes, pruning miles of hedges all leafing out in unison, and just keeping up with the watering in a drought. These controls help us to keep the gardens ready for maximum enjoyment during our relatively short summer and able to look picture-perfect for the garden events everyone wants to plan during that verdant time.

When feeling bogged down by these responsibilities, I always find solace in stepping into our own garden to work with the plants and the soil for a few minutes, to remind me of this very important connection I must maintain with the earth.

Russell, as Head Gardener, would say similarly that allowing a garden space to evolve is one of the greatest joys of our profession. It is a labor of observation that comes from familiarizing and immersing yourself in a piece of land. Be open to necessary change. What has worked for years may no longer make cultural or aesthetic sense. Always remember the original intent for a space—is it supposed to be calming, energizing, shady, sunny? A well-crafted garden needs to inspire, to welcome visitors—and most important to ask them, without words, to pause. A well-designed garden communicates the opportunity to appreciate details as well as the overall mood. Gardens are anything but static, so maintenance plans cannot be formulaic. Real care converts a designed plant collection into a "community" of plants that are comfortable in their setting.

He'd say a view from a bench can inspire the visitor to move deeper into a garden. An intimate experience along that route might be hidden at first by a large-scale player, adding a surprise. At the farthest point of the garden path, the reverse view might be anchored by that bench, giving the visitor a sense that they've taken a comfortable and pleasant journey; they feel oriented even in a densely planted, enveloping space. This circular experience of travel through a large garden can capture exquisitely memorable, detailed moments and create an overwhelming feeling of complete serenity in the soul. Often, we cannot articulate this, but internally we feel "calm." Engineering these moments is blissful.

When space is at a premium, conversely, how it will be used is critical. While we are designing, we are often inspired to create the most intimate of experiences. Small spaces challenge us to crystallize our thoughts; the constraint forces us to get the placement of all the ingredients just right. It is fun to select individual plant specimens and utilize them as objects along with the "hardgoods"—ornaments, containers, and focal points. Often small spaces juxtapose the indoors and outdoors, making the experience cohesive and dynamic. Russell always advocates for "shopping at home" by dividing or propagating an existing plant and introducing it in other "garden rooms" on the property; some repetition smooths transitions.

Good gardening practices come not only from textbooks; Russell also says that learning from experienced people has been the most important contributor to his methods. Learning never ends. It is wise to take advantage of every opportunity to gather new knowledge from an expert. Base knowledge combined with critical thought drawn from observation of unique conditions and aesthetics allows us to immerse ourselves into what a space is saying. We all think about what to do in next year's garden through the winter months (hopefully in front of a cozy, wood-burning stove), but Russell would argue that true evaluation is not so seasonal—that it's better to act on the changes that come as revelations while they're fresh. Continued gardening over the course of the year has allowed us to learn to reflect about the way the space is developing. Russell also recommends spending time in a garden at different times of the day or in an "off" season to experience the shadows of the differing levels and angles of light. To pause periodically and analyze the geometry, colors, and combinations, how they play in the light, how plants interact. Who (which plant) is too aggressive is always a major concern. Managing them keeps balance. Predicting plant performance is as much a part of his design consideration as creating short-term beauty.

Pulling yourself away from the urgent, ongoing maintenance tasks that every garden presents is hard. The planting, the weeding, the staking, the deadheading—all are necessary, but so is contemplation. Try to discipline yourself to have a little of both happen at the same time. The whole point of a garden is to capture how a space feels at different moments throughout the year, and most change daily in minute ways that we miss if we forget to stop and enjoy them. Russell advocates getting your hands dirty while you're contemplating. Connection with the physical helps the mental. He isn't afraid to be the muddiest person in the garden! With our staff as with our clients and indeed our gardens, we encourage self-determination, self-sufficiency, and growth. This continues as we observe the changes that time brings to each. Gardening is more than the horticultural development of a space—it's about creating a personal relationship with nature, whatever our "official position" relative to a garden. Gardening, like life, is dynamic.

We have grown old with many of our gardens, and in that time, we and they have developed a patina bestowed by age that we prize and hope others will as well.

—Craig Bergmann

In the English Tradition

Wrought iron intertwined with live pear foliage.

At some moment, every landscape designer working in America realizes how much our own tradition owes to English garden style and wants to learn about that history. In the firm's early days, we felt that pull, and in the early 1980s, we made the pilgrimage to the Chelsea Flower Show and scheduled a garden tour drive-about. We were hooked. Few experiences in life can compare to seeing Great Dixter, Sissinghurst, Kiftsgate Court Gardens, the Longstock Park Water Garden, or the RHS garden at Wisley for the first time. There have been many subsequent trips where various members of the company have travelled to see garden masterpieces in person, the popular as well as the private.

These classic English gardens inspire us and deepen a love of period architecture and the patina that can only be earned with time on a scale that's measured in centuries, not years or even decades. The combination creates a present beauty while emphasizing historical importance, a floriferous and verdant environment unlike anything we can experience here. The Arts and Crafts period, in particular, was addictive in integrating the built and the natural worlds so beautifully. This now-familiar style of gardening pioneered contrasting formal geometry and heavy masonry details with naturalistic, effusive, loose planting, and we apply a similar tactic in our work now.

These trips also taught a key principle: the best gardens clearly reflect the tastes or personalities of their maker or owner. A true passion for gardening—at any scale—is omnipresent on this green island, emboldening self-expression and experimentation. That first tour made it clear that good gardens are only half about plants; their other half has everything to do with the people who create and care for them. In that way, the simple cottages and wooded spaces of the countryside could seem equally as well-thought-out as the large manors where it was clear that someone had placed an occasional *Campanula* or *Erysimum* to grow out of a wall just so.

We have been so lucky on our garden-centric trips. At the urging of our English garden designer friend Stephen Woodhams, Craig spent an afternoon weeding with Christopher Lloyd and his Dachshunds, Tulipa and Dahlia, after asking if Christopher could use some help. Surreal! Russ and Deanna ventured to Great Dixter on their own virgin voyage to the United Kindgom, and while they were walking through, a man shouted out from across the garden, "Hey Russ, Deanna! What are you doing here?" They turned to see Fergus Garrett, the chief executive. What unbelievable fortune. At Craig's invitation, Fergus and Christopher Lloyd had visited The Country Garden a few years earlier and had loved touring behind the scenes. But we couldn't believe he would recognize any of us again, let alone from across the garden. He gave then them an impromptu walk through the whole facility. Similarly, an introduction to Rosemary Verey from our dear friend Posy Krehbiel from Lake Forest produced an invitation to lunch in her garden at Barnsley House. And on a fluke, John Brookes happened to be in his elegantly casual garden at Denmans when some of us stopped by, and we struck up a friendship that lasted until his passing years later.

Waking early to avoid the congestion fee in London, Russ and Deanna were up and out another morning before seven o'clock. This happily allowed them to arrive at Beth Chatto's Gravel Garden in Essex just at opening. It was a damp, crisp morning, and they were the first visitors. Because the trip was a whirlwind of hiking and touring, they had been using gas-filled trekking poles. They had paused to admire the hebe when a gardener carrying a woven trug walked up with a lady beside him and inquired about the poles—it was Beth herself! After chatting a bit, she asked their opinion on the pond area and what they would do with it. They will never forget that moment. Upon learning they had no firm plans, the gardener took time out of his day to show them a few interesting places nearby. The lesson for us in these great places was that all gardeners would do well to adopt this particularly British spirit of generosity.

A Timeless Tudor

Our bent for English-inspired, exuberant herbaceous garden design drew this client to us. This wonderful Tudor house in Hinsdale, a lush suburb west of Chicago filled with beautiful old houses, had something truly unique going for it: The original owner worked on LaSalle Street, and when the road was being converted from brick to paving in the 1920s, he bargained for the bricks and used them as the main building blocks for this house, the coach house, driveways, and perimeter garden walls. To them he added salvaged sixteenth-century English Tudor architectural timbers, doors, and moldings. What was officially new construction immediately took on the feel of an English country house. It was our job to create a garden befitting this evocative, meticulous design.

The space is clearly defined by the surrounding walls, an enclosure intended to help create more forgiving microclimates for plants and to protect them from typical four-legged pests—resident Dachshunds also kept any mice at bay. It was exciting for us to create a space where roses, lilies, and asters could thrive without having to battle ravishing rabbits. An original rill in the sunken courtyard needed restoration, but overall, this traditional layout gave us the perfect setting for a classic herbaceous perennial garden. The owners had a passion for growing cut flower varieties, and we indulged them with species from across the spectrum: peonies, delphiniums, lilacs, old rose varieties, and a rainbow of seasonal dahlias and Salvias. Craig and Cathy Dammann reimagined the circulation through the space with a narrow path of reclaimed brick pavers that allowed us to expand planting beds. To underscore the English mood, we added the quintessentially British plant 'Munstead' lavender as a hedge along the edge of the perimeter wall. It's planted in a sand trench for year-round drainage and protected from potential damage with a reclaimed-brick mow strip.

Off the garden room, we transformed a concrete-paver terrace with new local flagstone that adds much more interest and dimension, while paying careful attention to the mature honey locust tree at its center; it casts welcome shade over the house. The original planter boxes were also restored and placed on new stone steps leading to the garden room. To unify all garden spaces, we added box-edge cutting beds along the coach house's long foundation and installed a series of oak and iron arched trellises planted with romantic climbing roses along an existing brick walkway. The arch posts and strap iron detailing were modeled after the Deanery Garden pergola designed by the English architect Sir Edwin Lutyens in 1899.

In 1999, a decade or so after our initial intervention, the clients requested a lap pool; we settled it between the rose-arcade walkway and the main sunken garden, veiling it from the main house with a Belgian fence of espaliered pear and box hedging. A giant topiary box apple with a hand-wrought iron stem and leaf adds a touch of whimsy to keep the elegant space from taking itself too seriously. All of the continued Garden Care of this property, and the following garden, has been under the dedicated and highly skilled efforts of Roberto Hernandez.

Climbing roses cover the oak and strap-iron arches on the path from the cutting garden to the pool terrace.

The Sunken Garden behind the house features the restored rill and a fountain the client named *Unis*.

Espalier pear and boxwood soften the pool terrace wall, with a glazed terra-cotta jar, c. 1900, as a decorative element.

Overleaf: Planting plan for the Sunken Garden.

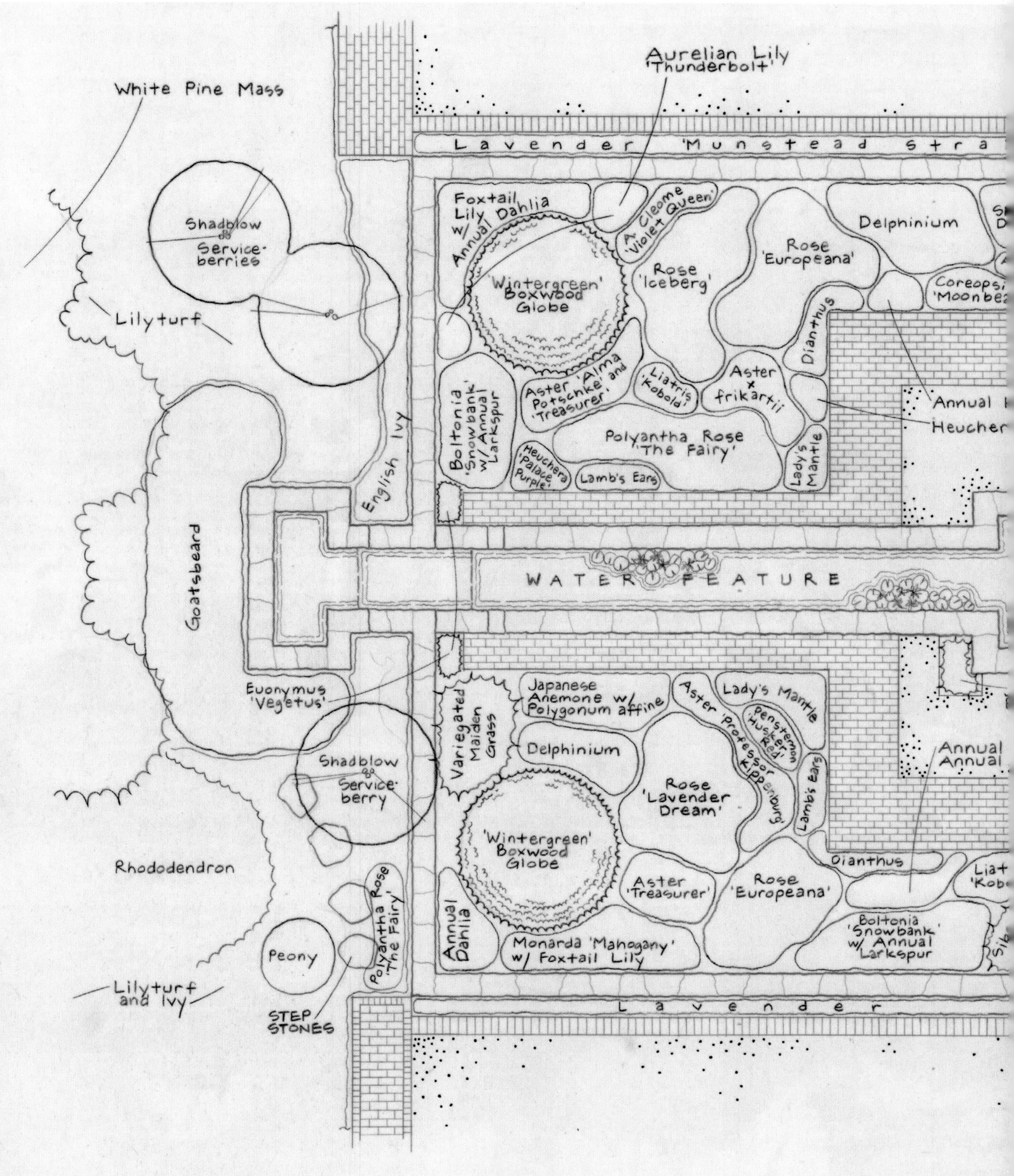

Scale: 1/4" = 1'-0"

Please Note: This is not a construction drawing.

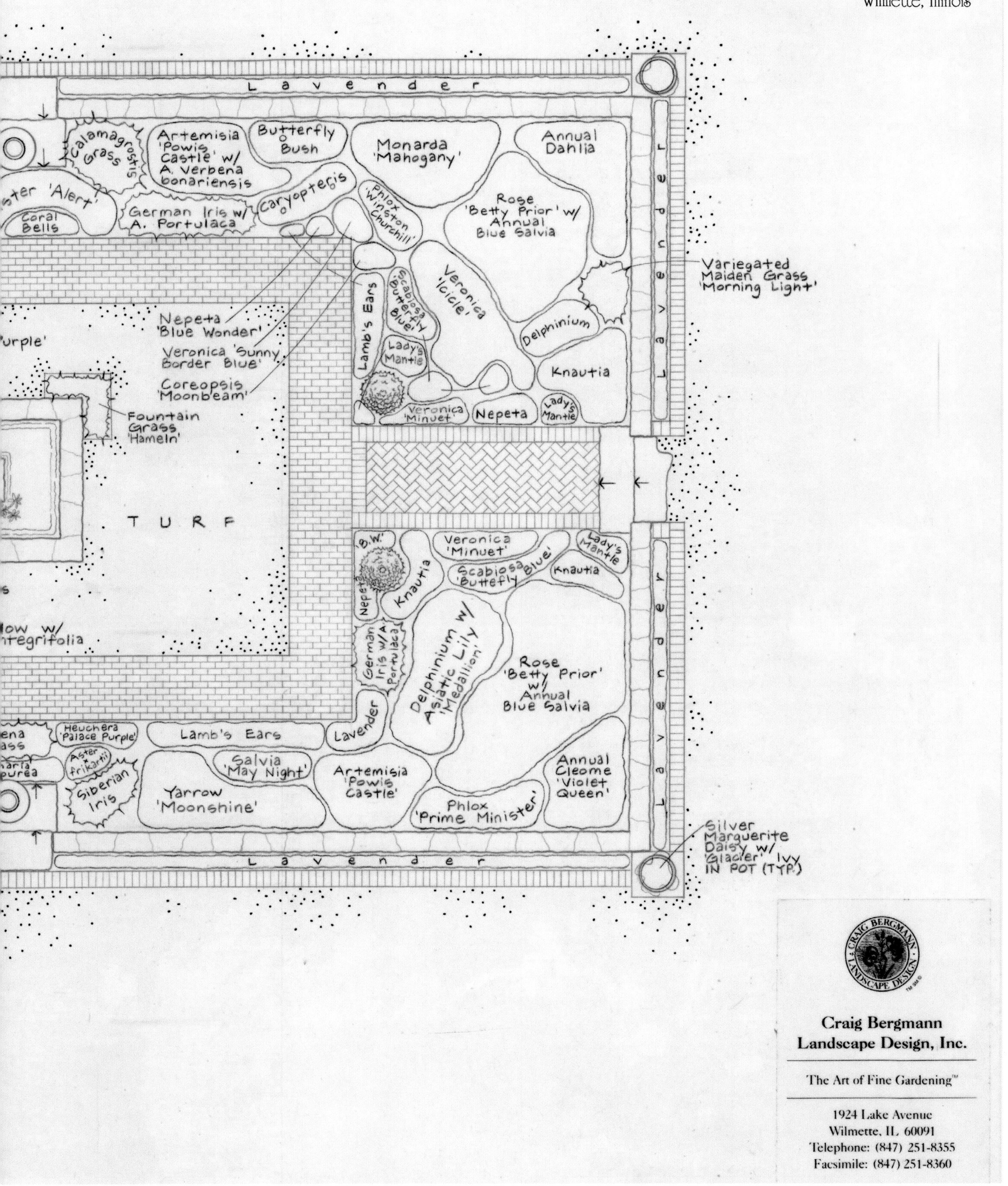
© 1994 Craig Bergmann Landscape Design Incorporated
Wilmette, Illinois
Lavender
Calamagrostis Grass
Artemisia 'Powis Castle' w/ A. Verbena bonariensis
Butterfly Bush
Monarda 'Mahogany'
Annual Dahlia
ster 'Alert'
Coral Bells
German Iris w/ A. Portulaca
Caryopteris
Phlox 'Winston Churchill'
Rose 'Betty Prior' w/ Annual Blue Salvia
Variegated Maiden Grass 'Morning Light'
Lamb's Ears
Scabiosa 'Butterfly Blue'
Veronica 'Icicle'
Delphinium
Nepeta 'Blue Wonder'
Veronica 'Sunny Border Blue'
Coreopsis 'Moonbeam'
'urple'
Lady's Mantle
Knautia
Fountain Grass 'Hameln'
Veronica 'Minuet'
Nepeta
Lady's Mantle
TURF
B.W.
Veronica 'Minuet'
Lady's Mantle
Scabiosa 'Butterfly Blue'
Knautia
Nepeta
Knautia
ow w/
ntegrifolia
German Iris w/A Portulaca
Delphinium w/ Asiatic Lily 'Medallion'
Rose 'Betty Prior' w/ Annual Blue Salvia
ena
ass
Heuchera 'Palace Purple'
Lamb's Ears
Lavender
Aster frikartii
Salvia 'May Night'
Artemisia 'Powis Castle'
Annual Cleome 'Violet Queen'
Siberian Iris
Yarrow 'Moonshine'
Phlox 'Prime Minister'
Silver Marguerite Daisy w/ 'Glacier' Ivy IN POT (TYP.)
Craig Bergmann Landscape Design
Craig Bergmann
Landscape Design, Inc.
The Art of Fine Gardening™
1924 Lake Avenue
Wilmette, IL 60091
Telephone: (847) 251-8355
Facsimile: (847) 251-8360

Previous spread: View across Sunken Garden with its *Lavendula* 'Munstead' surround.

Below: Summer planting in the rill. ***Opposite:*** An English lead container filled with Caladiums and a boot scrape animate the entry to the house.

Stone Manor

The inspiration for the architectural style of this house and the formal garden elements came directly from the clients' love of European travel. They aimed to re-create at a smaller scale some of the best details from the great estates and gardens they had visited—a dream project for all involved. Their unwavering enthusiasm and trust made us work even harder and more creatively to help this dream come true, and perhaps we were also encouraged by the numerous festivities they organized throughout the build process for our entire team and their families.

The landscape design, which organized the green spaces and specified the plant selection, was completed preconstruction. This gave us the luxury of two full years while the house was being built to find specimen plant materials, to grow specialty herbaceous perennials, and to source just the right antique garden ornaments and containers. Donald Bolak and Craig designed a complex green gallery space to highlight these collected treasures. The rear stone wall melds with an arbor structure designed specifically to support a massive Kentucky wisteria—decadently beautiful but also functional; it screens more of the adjoining property than a wall could alone.

The focus was to highlight the beauty of the masonry details and craftsmanship of all the structures, designed by R. Michael Graham of Liederbach & Graham Architects and built by Josef Masonry, by emphasizing its stateliness with a well-appointed garden. If we were successful in making it look historic, we did our job of incorporating several high-tech features needed to keep up the illusion while taking realities into account. Due to the local climate and particularities of the site, storm water management was a major challenge, but we worked diligently to conceal the mechanical elements involved, including installing underground vaults connected to the municipal sewer system at the front of the property. We hid one by placing a rose garden with a rill fountain and a *Taxodium* allée right atop it. Preserving every tree on this property was a priority, so mature specimens were protected to their driplines where possible, and we avoided trenching in the tender root zones by auguring all utilities. Geothermal pavement heating allows nearby plantings to avoid the wrath of snowplowing; to keep the plants from thinking they are experiencing a spring thaw in the middle of winter, we installed a two-inch-thick insulation board between the paving and soil to help mitigate the temperature change. The clients asked us to make everything at ground level beautiful with color, color, color. Happily, we had worked with them before, so we already knew their passion for rich, refreshing jewel tones in flower and foliage. An intense color scheme was great fun for us to concoct since many clients prefer more subdued palettes. And it's an extra pleasure for us to know that this garden is enjoyed not only by the owners, but also by the many guests they entertain at events throughout the year. That also means, however, that this garden must be "party ready" at all times. Since there is an ebb and flow to any garden's bloom timing, we gave extra consideration to details like enhancing the spring season's permanent plant collection with an extensive bulb layer for early color to bridge the gap before the herbaceous layer's blooms emerge. In summer the garden must seem to be at peak color continuously. To achieve that, we inserted planting pockets within the garden that allow us to integrate plants that are spectacular in shorter bursts and provide a longer bloom display through fall. The predominantly evergreen surround offers plenty of shapes for winter interest even if covered in snow, a green backdrop for the various gardens, and permanent structure for the landscape. This, in combination with the architecture of the woody plant collection, provides year-round interest in a garden that is always ready to receive.

South garage gable above towering *Taxodium distichum* 'Shawnee Brave'.

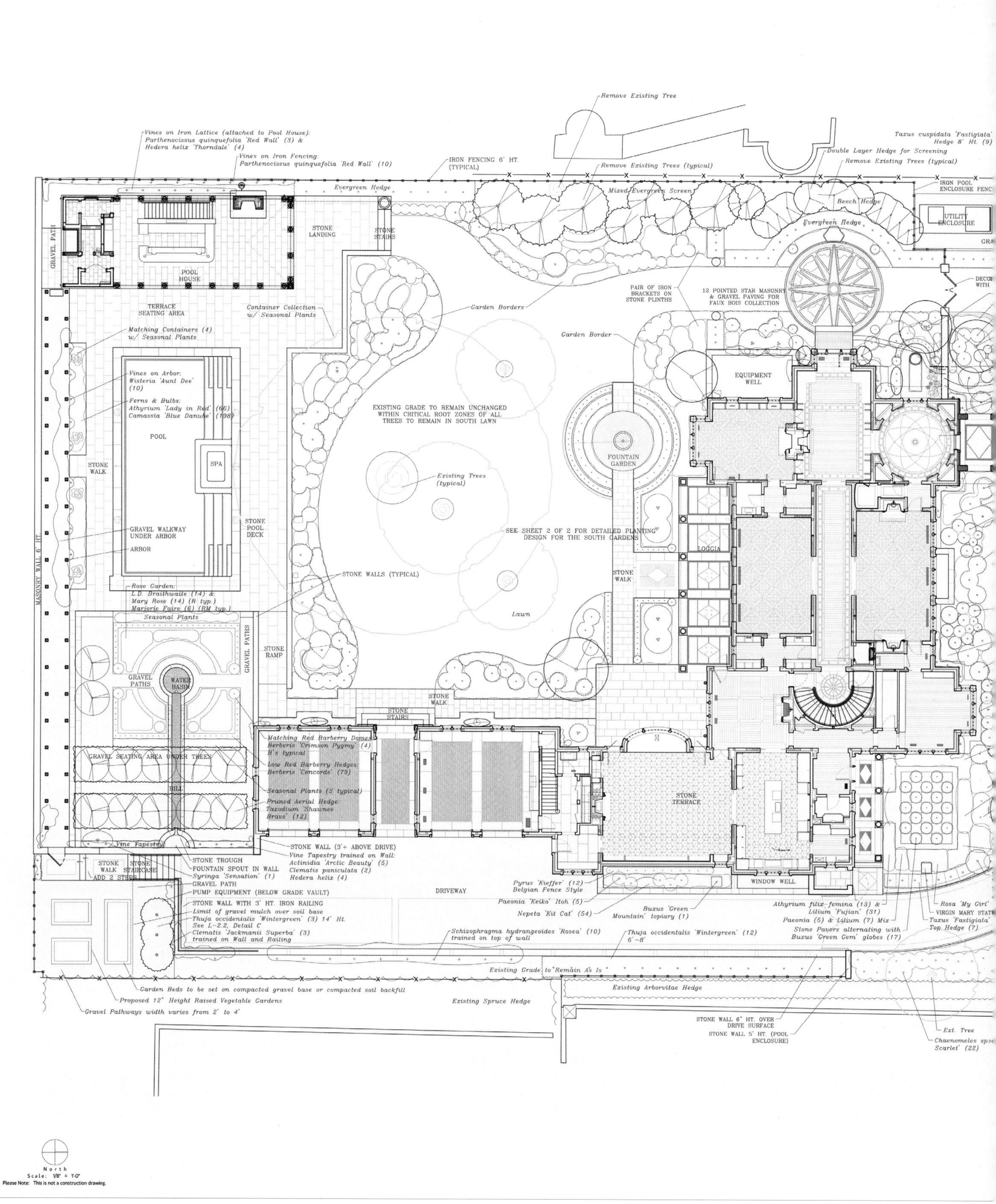

Remove Existing Tree
Vines on Iron Lattice (attached to Pool House):
Parthenocissus quinquefolia 'Red Wall' (3) &
Hedera helix 'Thorndale' (4)
Vines on Iron Fencing:
Parthenocissus quinquefolia 'Red Wall' (10)
IRON FENCING 6' HT.
(TYPICAL)
Remove Existing Trees (typical)
Taxus cuspidata 'Fastigiata'
Hedge 8' Ht. (9)
Double Layer Hedge for Screening
Remove Existing Trees (typical)
IRON POOL
ENCLOSURE FENC
Evergreen Hedge
Mixed Evergreen Screen
Beech Hedge
UTILITY
ENCLOSURE
Evergreen Hedge
GRAVEL PATH
POOL
HOUSE
STONE
LANDING
STONE
STAIRS
TERRACE
SEATING AREA
Container Collection
w/ Seasonal Plants
Garden Borders
PAIR OF IRON
BRACKETS ON
STONE PLINTHS
12 POINTED STAR MASONRY
& GRAVEL PAVING FOR
FAUX BOIS COLLECTION
Matching Containers (4)
w/ Seasonal Plants
Garden Border
Vines on Arbor:
Wisteria 'Aunt Dee'
(10)
Ferns & Bulbs:
Athyrium 'Lady in Red' (66)
Camassia 'Blue Danube' (198)
EQUIPMENT
WELL
EXISTING GRADE TO REMAIN UNCHANGED
WITHIN CRITICAL ROOT ZONES OF ALL
TREES TO REMAIN IN SOUTH LAWN
POOL
SPA
STONE
WALK
FOUNTAIN
GARDEN
Existing Trees
(typical)
STONE
POOL
DECK
GRAVEL WALKWAY
UNDER ARBOR
ARBOR
SEE SHEET 2 OF 2 FOR DETAILED PLANTING
DESIGN FOR THE SOUTH GARDENS
MASONRY WALL 6' HT.
LOGGIA
STONE WALLS (TYPICAL)
STONE
WALK
Rose Garden:
L.D. Braithwaite (14) &
Mary Rose (14) (R typ.)
Marjorie Fair (6) (RM typ.)
Seasonal Plants
Lawn
GRAVEL PATHS
STONE
RAMP
GRAVEL
PATHS
WATER
BASIN
STONE
WALK
STONE
STAIRS
Matching Red Barberry Domes:
Berberis 'Crimson Pygmy' (4)
B's typical
GRAVEL SEATING AREA UNDER TREES
Low Red Barberry Hedges:
Berberis 'Concorde' (79)
Seasonal Plants (S typical)
Pruned Aerial Hedge:
Taxodium 'Shawnee
Brave' (12)
STONE
TERRACE
Vine Tapestry
STONE WALL (3'+ ABOVE DRIVE)
Vine Tapestry trained on Wall:
Actinidia 'Arctic Beauty' (5)
Clematis paniculata (2)
Hedera helix (4)
STONE
WALK
STONE
STAIRCASE
ADD 2 STEPS
STONE TROUGH
FOUNTAIN SPOUT IN WALL
Syringa 'Sensation' (1)
GRAVEL PATH
PUMP EQUIPMENT (BELOW GRADE VAULT)
DRIVEWAY
Pyrus 'Kieffer' (12)
Belgian Fence Style
WINDOW WELL
STONE WALL WITH 3' HT. IRON RAILING
Limit of gravel mulch over soil base
Thuja occidentalis 'Wintergreen' (3) 14' Ht.
See L-2.2, Detail C
Clematis 'Jackmanii Superba' (3)
trained on Wall and Railing
Paeonia 'Keiko' Itoh (5)
Nepeta 'Kit Cat' (54)
Buxus 'Green
Mountain' topiary (1)
Athyrium filix-femina (13) &
Lilium 'Fujian' (31)
Paeonia (5) & Lilium (7) Mix
Stone Pavers alternating with
Buxus 'Green Gem' globes (17)
Rosa 'My Girl'
VIRGIN MARY STAT
Taxus 'Fastigiata'
Top Hedge (7)
Schizophragma hydrangeoides 'Rosea' (10)
trained on top of wall
Thuja occidentalis 'Wintergreen' (12)
6'-8'
Existing Grade to Remain As Is
Garden Beds to be set on compacted gravel base or compacted soil backfill
Proposed 12" Height Raised Vegetable Gardens
Gravel Pathways width varies from 2' to 4'
Existing Arborvitae Hedge
Existing Spruce Hedge
STONE WALL 6" HT. OVER
DRIVE SURFACE
STONE WALL 5' HT. (POOL
ENCLOSURE)
Ext. Tree
Chaenomeles spe
Scarlet' (22)
North
Scale: 1/8" = 1'-0"
Please Note: This is not a construction drawing.

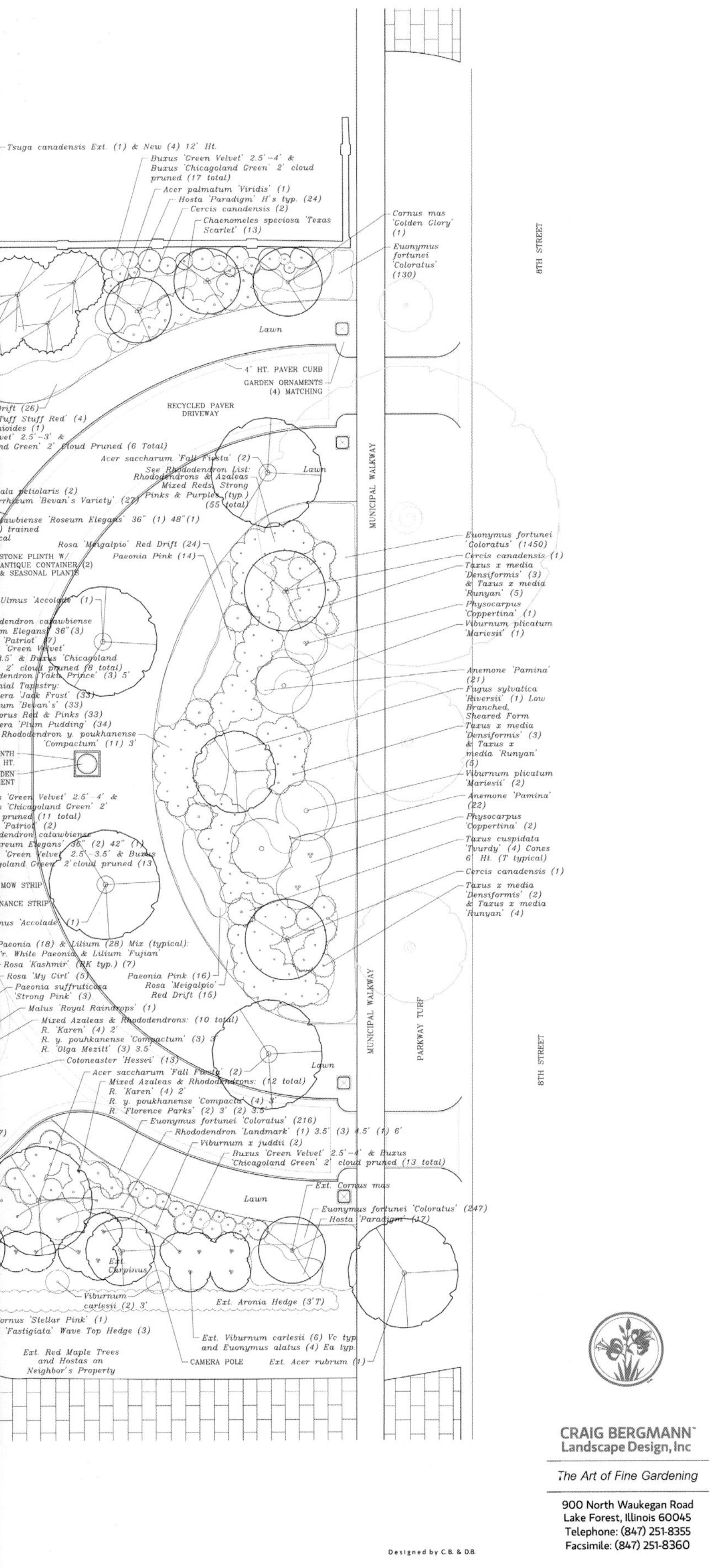

Landscape master plan.

Top left: *Lilium* 'Black Beauty' and a collection of planted containers soften the edges of the pool terrace. ***Bottom left:*** View from front porch to Rhododendrons in the spring.

Right: Entry piers and view to the front entry.

Top left: A compass rose enhances the rondel entry to the main garden.
Bottom left: A moss-furred stone lion at the corner of the kitchen terrace.

Right: The central fountain in the rose garden, complemented by *Ageratum houstonianum* 'Blue Horizon'.

Artful Collaboration

When Craig met the owners of this property at another garden in town, learned that they were the stewards of a historic Howard Van Doren Shaw house, and discovered that they had already engaged the renowned British designer Rosemary Verey to create a master plan for the estate grounds, he jumped at the chance to take them on as clients. The first time he drove up the gravel driveway to the elegant property, in 1989, he knew it was going to be a rare and wonderful commission. Both Craig and the clients had had the pleasure of visiting Barnsley House, her home and garden, in the Cotswolds. Craig also counted Rosemary as a friend; she had featured his personal garden in her book *The American Man's Garden*. He was determined to do justice, therefore, to her vision while ensuring that the grounds met current needs.

For a garden space south of the main house, the Lilac Room (so named because it incorporated the remains of a perimeter lilac hedge), Rosemary insisted that Craig collaborate on plant selection. As a local, he could select climate-appropriate species and then install and maintain the new garden. As the years passed, it became clear that the Lilac Room required careful consideration of seasonal flowers for continuous bloom so that there would always be an attractive display for the owners' short weekend stays between spring and fall. Bulbs such as *Narcissus, Muscari,* and *Allium* are interplanted with *Hydrangea, Paeonia,* and variegated *Miscanthus. Digitalis* is nestled in along the steppers, then later replaced with *Dahlias* for late summer bloom. Perennial delphinium leans on seasonal *Verbena bonariensis* and *Salvias* for support. Tulip 'White Triumphator' is planted for succession to the always-desired seasonal blue of *Ageratum. Cosmos bipinnatus* 'Sonata White' is placed at the front edge, alongside *Alchemilla* and *Veronica*. Burgundy notes are interjected for balance with *Heuchera, Cotinus,* and Japanese maple. To give accent, a tall, shiny herbaceous *Hibiscus*, 'Costa Rica', was planted for color balance near the *Baptisia*. It was a pleasure to revisit the garden periodically with Rosemary over the years as we continued to refine the garden. Rosemary, who passed in 2001, lives on here and her mark is indelible.

Since the initial installation, of course, there have been changes. An iron chain festoon, conceived and designed by CBLD, offers a glimpse of the garden over the entry drive hedges on one side and the pleached hornbeam–enclosed pool garden opposite. Russell has been particularly instrumental in keeping the English intent alive and well over the past thirty years, which has always been our quest. It also proves once again that the relationships of the people and the plants reveal artistic expression—achievable with dedication, conviction, and a good bit of luck.

Even though this was a weekend retreat for the clients, they kept it top of mind. Upon their return from a European trip or a friend's garden, our phone would ring. One major change involved the client-driven idea of adding a wall to replace failing historic lilacs and to clearly divide the main garden from the east woodland. Detailed brickwork was an obvious choice to pair with the house, and we duplicated an original wrought-iron gate on the property to set into it. Inspired by a space at Camp Rosemary, a neighboring garden, they added an allée of London plane trees mulched with bluestone gravel and edged with reclaimed granite cobblestone; all this was installed beyond the new gate in the wall. This also helped to give a more human scale to this expansive part of the property. We also worked together to unify a collection of whitewashed terra-cotta pots of varying sizes by planting each with a boxwood sphere. It became the perfect aisle for their granddaughter's wedding ceremony.

After a trip to rural Massachusetts, the owner decided to erect a full-scale replica of a late eighteenth-century American folly in the Georgian style. We added a boxwood-enclosed vegetable (since transformed into an herb) garden to reference the gardening style of the period, reiterating that American estates had always combined productivity with beauty. The two-story folly also conceals pool equipment, and the second floor is a private remote office (or at least a place for smoking cigars) and a wonderful place for grandchildren to open Christmas morning presents under the tree.

Summer view across the Lilac Room to the east wall gate.

Below: Lilac Room tank (the English term for fountain) with the neoclassical folly in the distance. ***Opposite:*** A figure by Simon Verity nestled among *Eupatorium* and *Hydrangea*.

Overleaf: *Platanus x acerifolia* allée with a collection of potted box.

Above: Festoon in the Old Rose walk. ***Opposite:*** Central quartet of *Malus* 'Coralburst' in summer with English *Rosa* 'Graham Thomas' and *Alchemilla mollis*.

Overleaf: Late summer foliage and flower tapestry with blue *Helictotrichon sempervirens* and the graceful *Actaea simplex atropurpurea* beyond.

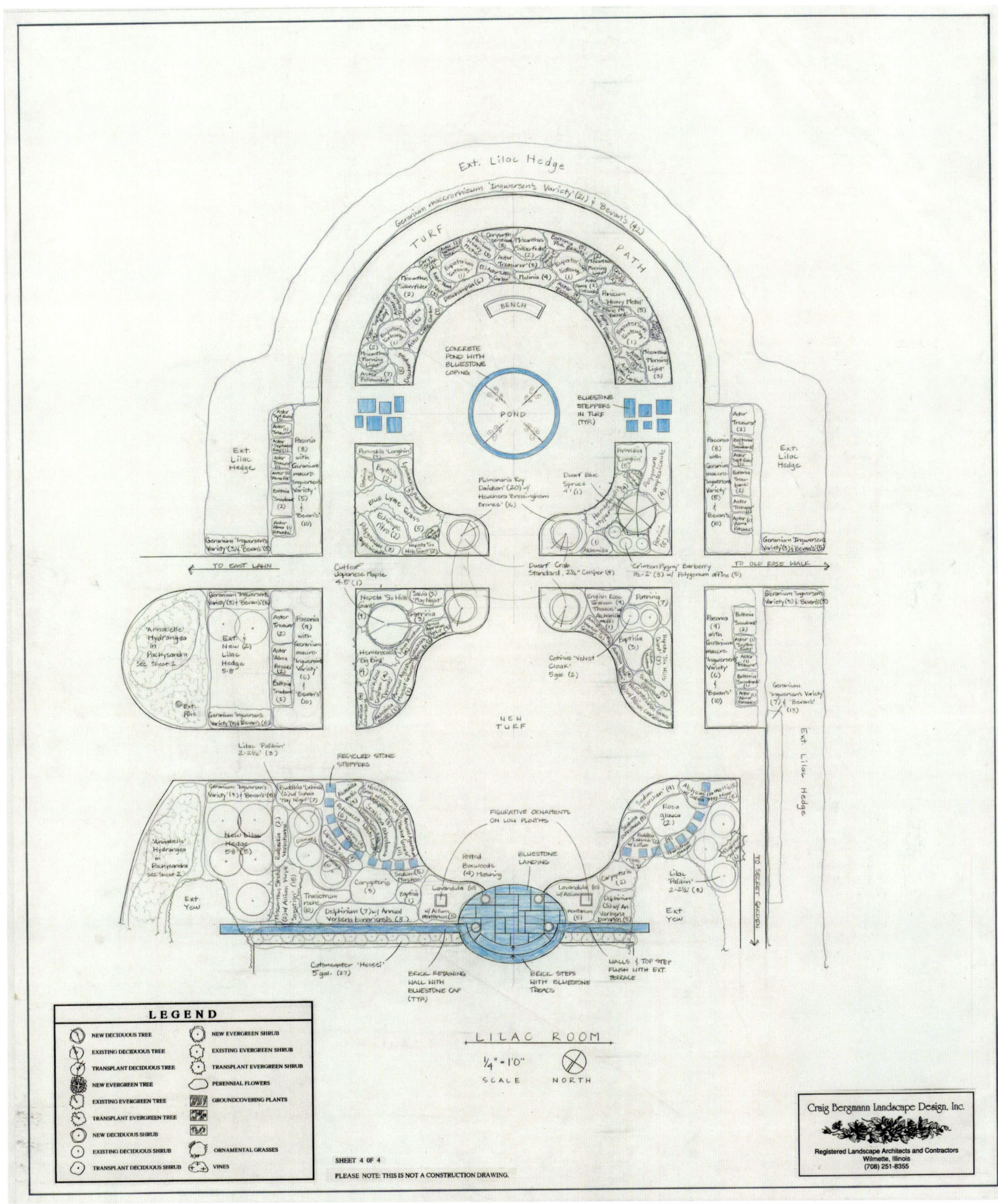

Opposite: Elliptical steps were introduced by breaking through the box edge from the original sunroom stone terrace to provide a garden entry to the Lilac Room. ***Above:*** Lilac Room planting plan.

Interpreting Arts and Crafts

This house, built in 2002, is modelled after Little Thakeham, a Lutyens design in the Arts and Crafts style. It was a collaboration between architect, interior designer, and landscape architect from the outset. Our approach to defining an appropriate and distinctive English garden style to complement the house was to reference all the best of this period: effusive foliage and flowers in an organized chaos and hardscape and ornamental elements that reference the building's details.

The house and its perimeter landscape wall in East Coast granite and tan Midwestern limestone set the tone for the site, even from the street. Reclaimed terra-cotta paving brick from Chicago city streets provides texture and history for the circular drive. The gravel entry court also feels period appropriate while concealing compensatory storm-water storage for progressive drainage to a natural ravine across the street.

Mature white oak trees at the front were preserved, and caliper inch-by-inch replacements of two heritage oaks felled for the construction were added. Both heritage oak trunks were milled, and their lumber was used for the pergola canopy and garden gates. It's always a goal to repurpose wonderful trees and keep them on site in some way if possible. Many other mature trees were preserved, even though that effort required planning the front walk around them with entry walls adjusted to accommodate their roots and steel plates used to span the wall as supports to avoid cutting the roots.

We also conceived a hand-wrought, iron-and-bronze arched tunnel to obscure the view of the garage court from the pool yard. It supports a series of three-tiered, palmetto verrier-espaliered Keiffer pears. The structure itself was sculpted with details of leaves and pears welded to give the impression that the allée is always leafed out and in fruit, regardless of season. The walkway underneath is detailed with alternating geometric forms designed by Charles Fischer to heighten the impression of length, and the fine craftsmanship of the masonry complements the house. To help the pears immediately fit the custom structure, we grew them on the inside of a hoop house with a similar curvature to train them before installation.

Repurposed excess terra-cotta roof tiles were imbedded into garden walls and paving to mimic the Lutyens-esque details in the main house. Collected antique containers and objects amassed during the muti-year build allowed us to "age" the finished landscape with objects that harken to the past, strengthening visual ties between garden and house.

In the plant realm, favorite jewel-toned herbaceous plants abound in the designated garden areas including *Delphinium, Peonia, Dahlias,* and roses at center stage. Cultivars of native plants including crimson *Monarda* and *Amsonia* provide height and dramatic foliage effect. Towering *Arundo donax* grass and butterfly bushes increase the scale of the pool border. We also snugged a sphere garden of rounded boxwood and spherical ornaments next to a diverse mixed border near the pool and the main lawn (included for children's play and compensatory storm water runoff). A vine-covered stone entablature and a timbered canopy made of an oak from the site, now covered in trumpet vine, at the main terrace provides a veil from the lawn activities and provides much-needed afternoon shade.

Now fully established in this mature neighborhood, the house has settled in well and is one of the most verdant spots on the block. Each spring the species tulips that were in the landscape long before the owners purchased it bloom again, in proud contrast with the new Virginia bluebells and hellebores, also self-seeding gradually. Trees amending the site cast beckoning shade for passersby in the heat of summer while climbing hydrangea vines clambering over the front stone walls observe those seeking a glimpse into the green beyond.

Wrought-iron tunnel with iron leaves, branches, and bronze pears, supporting candelabra espalier *Pyrus communis* 'Keiffer'.

Opposite: The paved entry drive of reclaimed street brick leads to the house designed by architect R. Michael Graham. ***Above:*** A secret garden gate in wall with terra-cotta rooftile and reclaimed keystone detailing.

Above: The Sphere Garden. ***Right:*** Pool Garden with *Amsonia hubrichtii* and *Solenostemon scut.* 'Big Red' with a view to a pair of Scottish stone obelisks.

Overleaf: Jewel tones of *Delphinium*, *Rosa* 'Salita', *Phormium* 'Flamingo', *Cotinus coggygria* 'Velvet Cloak' with *Arundo donax* and *Rosa rubrifolia* in the pool garden.

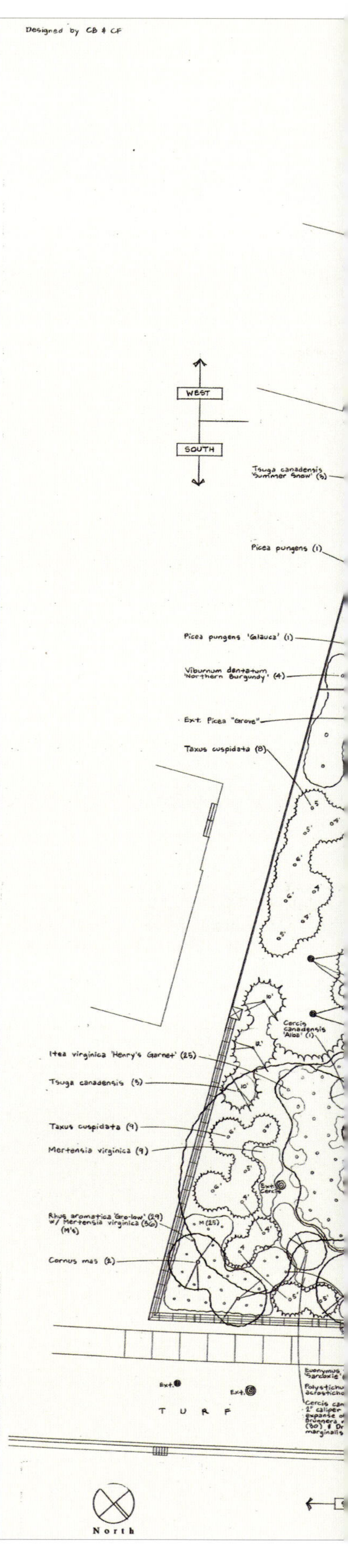

Above: A secluded terrace with potted palms and Begonia outside the office on the lower level. Right: Master plan.

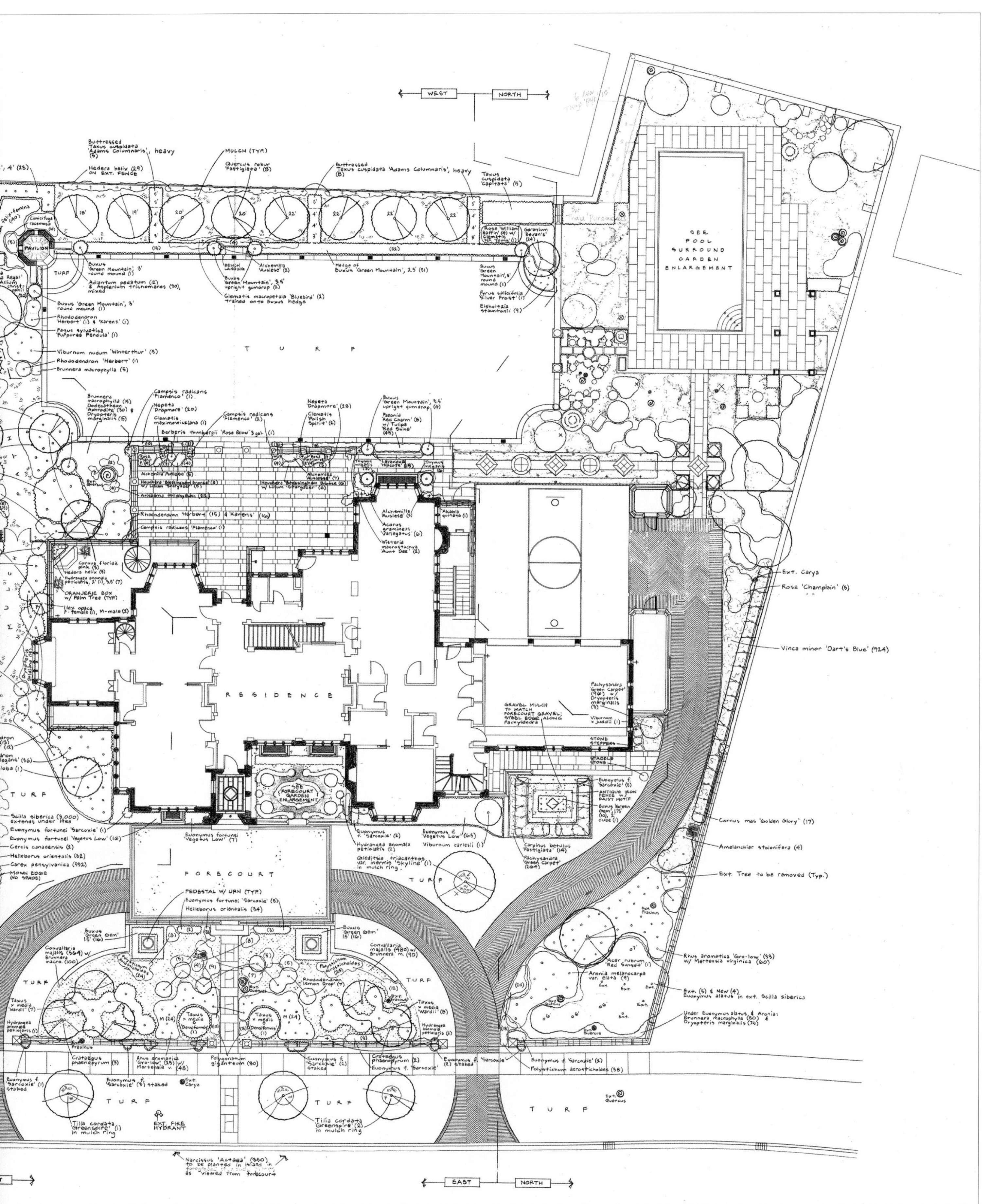

WEST
NORTH
Buttressed Taxus cuspidata 'Adams Columnaris', heavy (8)
MULCH (TYP.)
Quercus robur 'Fastigiata' (8)
Buttressed Taxus cuspidata 'Adams Columnaris', heavy (8)
Hedera helix (29) ON EXT. FENCE
Taxus cuspidata 'Capitata' (5)
PAVILION
TURF
Buxus 'Green Mountain', 3' round mound (1)
Adiantum pedatum (12) & Asplenium trichomanes (30), mixed
BENCH LANDING
Alchemilla 'Auslese' (2)
Buxus 'Green Mountain', 3.5' upright gumdrop (2)
Hedge of Buxus 'Green Mountain', 2.5' (51)
Clematis macropetala 'Bluebird' (2) trained onto Buxus hedge
Buxus 'Green Mountain', 3' round mound (1)
Rhododendron 'Herbert' (1) & 'Karens' (1)
Fagus sylvatica 'Purpurea Pendula' (1)
Viburnum nudum 'Winterthur' (5)
Rhododendron 'Herbert' (1)
Brunnera macrophylla (5)
Pyrus salicifolia 'Silver Frost' (1)
Elsholtzia stauntonii (9)
SEE POOL SURROUND GARDEN ENLARGEMENT
T U R F
Brunnera macrophylla (15) Dodecatheon 'Aphrodite' (30) & Dryopteris marginalis (15)
Campsis radicans 'Flamenco' (1)
Nepeta 'Dropmore' (20)
Clematis maximowicziana (1)
Campsis radicans 'Flamenco' (2)
Nepeta 'Dropmore' (28)
Clematis 'Polish Spirit' (2)
Buxus 'Green Mountain', 3.5' upright gumdrop (4)
Paeonia 'Red Charm' (8) w/ Tulipa 'Red Shine' (48)
Berberis thunbergii 'Rose Glow' 3 gal. (1)
Alchemilla 'Auslese' (5)
Arisaema triphyllum (25)
Rhododendron 'Herbert' (15) & 'Karens' (16)
Campsis radicans 'Flamenco' (1)
Alchemilla 'Auslese' (3)
Acorus gramineus 'Variegatus' (6)
Wisteria macrostachya 'Aunt Dee' (2)
Akebia quinata (1)
Cornus florida, pink (3)
Hedera helix (3)
Hydrangea anomala petiolaris, 2' (1), 3.5' (7)
ORANJERIE BOX w/ Palm Tree (TYP.)
Ilex opaca F-female (6), M-male (2)
R E S I D E N C E
Ext. Carya
Rosa 'Champlain' (5)
Vinca minor 'Dart's Blue' (924)
Pachysandra 'Green Carpet' (90) w/ Dryopteris marginalis (3)
Viburnum x juddii (1)
GRAVEL MULCH TO MATCH FORECOURT GRAVEL; STEEL EDGE ALONG Pachysandra
STONE STEPPERS
STADDLE STONE
Euonymus f. 'Sarcoxie' (5)
ANTIQUE IRON FENCE w/ DAISY MOTIF
SEE FORECOURT GARDEN ENLARGEMENT
Cornus mas 'Golden Glory' (17)
Amelanchier stolonifera (4)
Ext. Tree to be removed (Typ.)
T U R F
Scilla siberica (3,000) extends under Ilex
Euonymus fortunei 'Sarcoxie' (1)
Euonymus fortunei 'Vegetus Low' (16)
Cercis canadensis (2)
Helleborus orientalis (32)
Carex pensylvanica (332)
MOWN EDGE (NO SPADE)
Euonymus fortunei 'Vegetus Low' (7)
Euonymus f. 'Sarcoxie' (2)
Hydrangea anomala petiolaris (2)
Euonymus f. 'Vegetus Low' (63)
Viburnum carlesii (1)
Carpinus betulus 'Fastigiata' (14)
Pachysandra 'Green Carpet' (264)
Gleditsia triacanthos var. inermis 'Skyline' (1) in mulch ring
F O R E C O U R T
PEDESTAL W/ URN (TYP.)
Euonymus fortunei 'Sarcoxie' (5)
Helleborus orientalis (34)
TURF
Buxus 'Green Gem' 15' (16)
Convallaria majalis (564) w/ Brunnera macro. (100)
Convallaria majalis (480) w/ Brunnera m. (90)
Rhododendron 'Lemon Drop' (9)
Taxus x media 'Wardii' (7)
Taxus x media 'Wardii' (8)
Taxus x media 'Densiformis' (1)
Rhus aromatica 'Gro-low' (33) w/ Mertensia virginica (60)
Acer rubrum 'Red Sunset' (1)
Aronia melanocarpa var. elata (9)
Ext. (5) & New (4) Euonymus alatus in ext. Scilla siberica
Under Euonymus alatus & Aronia: Brunnera macrophylla (50) & Dryopteris marginalis (75)
Crataegus phaenopyrum (3)
Rhus aromatica 'Gro-low' (25) w/ Mertensia v. (48)
Polygonatum giganteum (30)
Euonymus f. 'Sarcoxie' (2) staked
Crataegus phaenopyrum (2)
Euonymus f. 'Sarcoxie'
Euonymus f. 'Sarcoxie' (2)
Polystichum acrostichoides (38)
Euonymus f. 'Sarcoxie' (1) staked
Euonymus f. 'Sarcoxie' (3) staked
Ext. Carya
T U R F
Tilia cordata 'Greenspire' (1) in mulch ring
EXT. FIRE HYDRANT
Tilia cordata 'Greenspire' (2) in mulch ring
Ext. Quercus
Narcissus 'Actaea' (350) to be planted in island in foreground of forecourt as "viewed from forecourt"
EAST
NORTH

The Deerpath Inn

The first contact with the owners of this inn made our involvement seem inevitable. When Craig answered the call from the owners' corporate office, the CEO's first words were: "I hear that if I want an English garden in Illinois, you're the guy." Craig chimed right in, responding, "If you're talking about building an English-style garden here in town, you're right. If you're trying to install actual English plants in Illinois, you are going to fail." The call proceeded amicably, so Craig agreed to review preliminary plans for the total renovation of a Tudor-style inn last renovated in the 1940s by architect Stanley Anderson. Craig and Erin Marie Herrera researched many historic English inns for reference and inspiration on surrounding gardens, then set all aspects of the landscape architecture through the theoretical sieve for heavy public use and materials appropriate for Midwest conditions. The Deerpath Inn has since become a mainstay for special events and local dining in Lake Forest, saved by the major renovation.

One of the most immediately impactful ways to make a public space memorable is to create drama. We emphasized circulation through the grounds and created strong points of interest to keep visitors engaged. Flexibility was critical in planning the outdoor spaces to accommodate a variety of gatherings. We activated a vestibule entrance to the banquet facility by transforming it into an outdoor patio with a fireplace that also screens this zone from the street. We capped its flagstone wall with reclaimed terracotta roof tiles to link the new construction to the older building.

The main patio courtyard is surrounded on three ivy-covered sides by the inn; the fourth side borders condominiums, so we added a tall evergreen hedge for privacy. A life-size bronze stag presides over the courtyard, commissioned by the CEO to reference the name of the inn. The brick-and-limestone detailing of the building inspired our very English "crazy paving" of bluestone and complementary brick, arranged in what seems to be a random pattern. These materials, importantly, provide a relatively smooth surface for frequently changing furniture layouts and a stable base for tents erected in less-than-ideal weather situations. Stone planters and ornaments accessorize the patio and add interest to views for diners and guests staying at the inn.

The foundation planting incorporates the original Boston and English ivy that we saved during the renovation. A wave box hedge was added for a bit of whimsy, along with a tapestry of simple-but-interesting perennials and groundcovers that carpet the base.

The inn management also asked Craig to help stylize the interior of the Garden Room, a dining space set under a sort of glass conservatory and overlooking the patio. We searched our own inventory of antiques and even shopped the brocante areas of local garden centers looking for pieces that would carry through the English aesthetic. On the dining tables, vintage half-pint milk jars hold blended bouquets. Vintage wire, light-colored terra-cotta, and iron pieces to keep the look historic but casual to differentiate the space from the formal English Room, which Craig also helped to decorate. For the tables there, we repurposed silver mint julep cups as containers for *Calandiva* or mini orchids. A focal point display is composed of traditional materials that emphasize the room's grandeur: a large, mirrored planter box supports a stone faux-bois birdbath that holds three tall glass vases nestled into a collection of antlers. The vases are filled with tall, spring flowering or fall branches, foxglove, foxtail lilies—all often harvested from the Gardens at 900 or from the nursery.

Appealing to the broad audience of visitors and diners requires keeping arrangements of peak displays in every season. In addition to cut-flower bouquets, the Lobby, Hearth Room, and other public areas display a diverse collection of orchids. A favorite spot inside is what we call "the window seat," a wide ledge perfect for showcasing an ever-changing, charmingly mismatched collection of unique plant species often in patinated containers. The inn also periodically requests tabletop arrangements for Sunday brunches; for these we try to use "homey" containers that feel as if they have come out of grandma's curio cabinet. For the holidays, we transform the inn with Christmas trees, garlands, specialty flowers, and decorations. We're proud that floral displays have become synonymous with the inn's identity, and we continue to provide all these services for them to this day.

Bronze stag in the courtyard.

Above: Masonry details mark the entrance and integrate the public street with the sidewalk.

Opposite, top: Welcoming stone finials invite guests inside. ***Opposite, bottom:*** "Crazy paving" animates the dining courtyard.

Overleaf: Rendered plan of landscape spaces.

North
0
5'
10'
20'

Previous spread: Our Mother's Day display is a spring attraction for the inn.

Above: A Halloween display, by Russell and his team, features a life-sized pumpkin house, furnished inside and out.

Above: The subtle textures of carved stone and autumn squash.

Harvestable

In our designs, we always include plants that provide something to harvest for the home, and we enjoy stretching the definition of what "harvestable" can mean. People don't need a grand cutting garden to grow blooms that can be picked and displayed, nor does creating a garden with productivity in mind commit us to including a vegetable plot. An entire landscape can contribute foliage and flowers and fruits of visual interest. We emphasize the widely variable uses so many plants offer with both our staff and clients, and indeed thinking differently about the intended or end use of the plants within the spaces we design adds depth to the conversation about creating an artful garden.

All the most beautiful, established potagers include a mix of fruit and flowers, herbs and vegetables. Think of the way plant communities grow in nature: a mix of seasonal, perennial, large, and small plants always coexists. Such symbiosis, with each type of plant growing in tandem with the rhythm of the insect world, allows for pollination, bolsters disease resistance, and nurtures a stable growing environment. We have learned over the years to mix up plants—all will grow happier in the long run. We focus on companion planting, attracting beneficial insects throughout blossoming to generate an abundant harvest, and most important fostering good air circulation.

We have built harvest gardens from a few square feet to full-blown potagers on half an acre with espaliered fruit trees, berry patches, asparagus, and rhubarb. It's so much fun to plan these in the depths of winter since so many of the members of these typically fenced or walled gardens are seasonal. For the intrepid gardeners, we will add a cold frame, compost pile, and sometimes a chicken coop. We're constantly amazed at how much a 10-by-10-foot garden space can produce with a little forethought given to partner crops and succession planting. Since the pandemic, when having basics nearby felt reassuring on a primal level, we are almost always asked for space for cutting flowers, tomatoes, and basil. "Harvestables" can create such a pretty garden!

An expansive potager provides enough for the owners and a local food pantry.

Cultural Inspiration

Inspiration comes from many sources. It can stem from a client's quirky passion, the uniqueness of a site, or even a moment in history. Combining inspiring details with a plant palette that emphasizes the theme or style of the original elements on a property can result in gardens that feel wholly of a place and appropriately scaled—and therefore satisfying on an almost subconscious level.

We often use reclaimed or patinated hardscape elements when we repair patios and walls, for example. When there's a transition on a property or any structure or feature is removed or demolished, we can almost always find remnants worthy of reusing. Repurposing is at the heart of our philosophy. A glut of miscellaneous leftover stones, bricks, iron vent covers, and stone or metal reliefs can be turned into "crazy paving" for a whimsical walkway that will definitely be a conversation piece. Always, always more interesting than newly purchased matching pavers! We've deconstructed and reconstructed rooftile pillars that clients felt were no longer right for their space. And then topped them with leftover cedar beams to create pergola-like shade structures that attracted lichen and "aged" into the property unbelievably quickly. A pair of metal marquee entry canopies from the 1970s turned out to be a perfect archway roost for doves and chickens. Architectural remnants placed in cleverly rethought ways leads to the overall feeling of time periods crossing paths in an intriguing way. The accumulation of "things" is not always a bad thing, and good pieces from every and any era can coexist. Noticing the usefulness of everyday items for alternative purposes is an art, what we call "having more crayons in our box to play with."

All of us who care and work for properties with history feel strongly that we are merely the current caretakers of a significant place, so we carefully consider interventions to ensure they match the stature and eminence of the original. Old-variety roses, for example, are used for their natural aesthetic link to the past, but it doesn't hurt that all that breeding has resulted in durability, disease resistance, and incredible fragrance. Modern roses seldom carry all of these attributes—something is lost, and it's typically fragrance. Newer cultivars of still old-fashioned plants often take less maintenance in terms of spraying needs, staking, or pruning, so we take advantage of that when we can. We all remind ourselves regularly that we chose this profession to work in and with gardens, not just design them on paper, and we are happy to have soil under fingernails and stains on jean knees if it means we are doing good work that helps preserve worthy landscapes. We will also gladly work to landmark the exteriors of historic structures with the state to ensure their preservation. Many of our gardens have been added to the Garden Club of America archives at the Smithsonian Institution in Washington, D.C.

Weathered rot-resistant cypress stump with a huge tree fern, a staghorn fern, and collected non-hardy ferns in a shaded spot.

Midwest Mediterranean

The clients sat with this property for ten years before building on it, giving themselves time to learn how the light, wind, and weather acted upon this bluff overlooking Lake Michigan. The one constant that the water of Lake Michigan provides is extremes, and it's famous for creating highly variable microclimates—the temperature variation spans fifteen degrees even over a short distance, and winds can blow in erratic gusts of up to twenty miles per hour during the summer. We often create garden rooms to help temper these conditions on waterfront properties, but they are still extremely variable. In spring particularly, temperatures mimic England's slow-to-warm climate, and often plantings along the lake fall two full weeks behind bloom schedules just a few miles inland. So, when the clients decided to try to re-create their favorite destination, the French Mediterranean, architect Phillip Liederbach knew it would be wise to collaborate with Donald Bolak and Craig for almost a year as the plans developed, ensuring details to enhance that style could be executed seamlessly in the garden.

A screen planting of hedges and trees adds privacy and much-needed wind protection for fragile blooms, especially in early spring before trees and shrubs leaf out fully—the most sheltered areas of the garden spaces will always be the most colorful. The property also borders a historic cemetery on the north, so the owners planted a two-hundred-foot-long row of Norway spruce soon after purchasing the property, creating a tall green wall that has grown in nicely fourteen years later.

The Mediterranean gave the whole design team inspiration for masonry details and the plant palette. The resulting yellow-hued stone of the house and garden walls also inspired the property's name: La Maison Jaune. We echoed the sky-blue trim color so popular in the south of France in various Mediterranean-associated flowers including wisteria, clematis, lavender, and catmint. Dahlias, lilies, and roses fill the garden with effusive scale and fragrance throughout the summer. Nora Kennedy and her Garden Care team continue to select seasonal cut flowers that blend well with the permanent players.

A Regency-style stone bench placed at the edge of the bluff overlooking Lake Michigan.

Normally we eschew fabric weed barriers in garden beds, but here they were essential in the rear foundation plantings; we needed to use crushed seashell mulch from North Carolina as warming agent to help the plants thrive but mixed with the soil it would have made a mess, blowing everywhere. We cut holes in the fabric to plant through, and now we can grow German irises, cottage pinks, and Russian sage. The owners requested that we follow the practice of feng shui in our design, to emulate the flow of water from the front yard through the house and down to the lake and to redirect energy away from the cemetery. The impressive five-hundred-foot-long lakefront parcel provided many opportunities to create different views and routes to the lake, so we emphasized successive framed views to draw people through the property, as if floating. The entrance gates frame the approach; the architecture of the garage wings frames the entrance; the connecting arches to each garage wing frame seasonal accents of color in the plantings across the drive; the gate to the main garden frames the approach; the ironwork of the main path through the garden frames the view beyond the garden to the lake; and the balustrade wall frames the pool view.

A funicular transports visitors down from the top of the bluff to a small cedar deck, offering beach time without sandy feet. For those who prefer to walk, we also developed a turf ramp that leads down to a circular patio detailed like a nautical compass; a private reading nook with an endless view awaits. During construction, a number of sand lenses were found seeping through the bluff, causing potential instability issues; the solution was to bore them directionally so they could drain down to the beach. The main garden enclosures include stone balustrades, rustic wood and wire fencing, and the walls of adjoining buildings, all contributing heft that matches the house's stature. In another nod to Mediterranean style, a central crushed-seashell path features a carved stone wellhead repurposed as planter, surrounded by a nautilus-shell-inspired stone pattern conceived by Donald Bolak. A covered loggia adds an architectural element that directs views out over the pool terrace, main garden, and lawn—the grand lake and its broad horizon is always the main focal point, providing an oceanic experience in the middle of the country.

Opposite, top: The wellhead sits on a stone surround with joint patterns inspired by a chambered nautilus shell. *Opposite, bottom:* An Asian-inspired spa garden abuts the pool house.

Above: The greenhouse and the garden gate.

Above: Hand-crafted metal lanterns flank the opening to the formal garden.
Right: Rendered landscape plan.

Overleaf: High summer with clematis clad arches and a seashell path.

North
Scale: NTS

Above: The fire table is nestled in Nepeta and shrub roses.
Opposite, top: Seasonal Nasturtium softens stone terrace edges.

Opposite, bottom: Rill fountain with French eighteenth-century iron fountainheads and urn with the fall glory of *Acer x freemanii* 'Autumn Blaze'.

Moorish Influence

A schoolteacher and an engineer fell in love with this 1908 Arts and Crafts–style home by Howard Van Doren Shaw and have tended to it as carefully as they would a child for decades. They kept the Alhambra-inspired rills, fountains, and elegant water cascades in working order, and the husband found a Locke mower to use on the original lawn, maintaining both the lawn and the equipment himself. When they called us to perform some updates to the garden, we found that, thanks to their diligence, the treasured historic elements were functioning as originally intended so we could dive right into planting instead of spending time or budget on infrastructure.

Over the course of almost ten years, Craig and Charles Fischer worked together to update this historic space judiciously. The site is diagonally oriented southeast/northwest on a large, sloped lot. This provides wonderful light in the house throughout the day and helps summer breezes flow through the one-room-deep plan. The estate was originally planted with massive American elms, but all except one succumbed to Dutch elm disease long ago. The remaining patriarch sits at cross axis to the center of the existing Sunken Garden, almost completely shading a space originally intended to be sunny, so we reworked its plant palette. Just before the stairs to the lower level, we added four fastigiate *Carpinus* to mark a subtle border that delineates a transition to the lower garden. An existing zigzag stone path that once ran through a hybrid rose garden now traverses beds of herbaceous perennials including *Phlox, Stachys, Iris siberica, Nepeta,* and *Geranium; Rosa* 'White Fairy' is included as a nod to the historical garden. The perimeter beds are kept simple by contrast, to serve as visual backdrop, and include a palette of 'Annabelle' hydrangea, ferns, *Astilbe,* 'Casa Blanca' lilies, *Geranium,* and *Astrantia.* Two large containers of blue hydrangeas on the lower garden patio provide punctuation. *Clematis* 'Huldine' is trained along the top of the retaining wall to add eye-level interest.

The color scheme for the floral display of the upper and lower gardens was inspired by the crewel-embroidered upholstery of the canopy bed in the principal bedroom. The upper garden beds that frame the upper rill are flanked by wave-shaped boxwood hedges to continue the water theme, and these bed locations were moved farther away from the rill than the historic plan intended, to provide a wider view to the sunken garden beyond. We also redirected the existing stone path to abut the rill coping, to limit any potentially clogging cut-turf nuisance in the water. Plants include herbaceous *Salvia, Calamintha,* and *Perovskia;* these aromatic mint-family choices are less attractive to deer or rabbits.

A herd of resident deer was in the habit of visiting the site year-round, so part of our work was to deter them and stop destruction in the main garden areas. The deer-ravaged historical yew hedges were all but destroyed, so they had to be removed. We enclosed the sunken space with a narrow cultivar of hornbeam, intending them to grow to a mature width and a height of eight feet. Because they were planted on two-foot centers. they were planted bare root. As an interim barrier, we assembled a fence of eight-foot-tall rebar stakes with lateral rails every two vertical feet. This stopped the deer from pushing through the hornbeam saplings while allowing the light needed for them to grow rapidly.

The walk that runs parallel to the upper rill leads to a stone landing; steps with an ornamental iron rail lead up to a sort of promontory pointing to the terminus view; here a pair of figures set atop plinths spill water into separate pools flanking a curved, intimate patio. A stone bridge over the lower basin allows the visitor to establish an intimate connection to the rill and traverse the turf paths.

A historical iron gate leads to the Stroll Garden, as we've named the east garden space, which was a mere palimpsest of its former self when we arrived. Upon excavation, we found an intricate pattern of poured-in-place concrete bed edging that we repaired and re-leveled to restore its original configuration. We filled it in with perennials including variegated *Brunnera macrophylla* 'Langtrees', Japanese painted fern, variegated *Vinca minor* 'Ralph Shugert', Solomon's seal, and spring ephemerals including white daffodils, blue-flowering Spanish bluebells (to mimic the non-hardy English bluebells so popular in English Arts and Crafts fabrics) and grape hyacinths. 'Ivory Halo'

An early twentieth-century iron gate opens into the Stroll Garden, originally designed by Rose Standish Nichols.

dogwood shrubs and more 'Incrediball' hydrangeas provide pops of white in the garden throughout the summer. A bronze sculpture of a potter found in the house now marks the far end of the garden. To the west is a stone archway etched with an inscription by Italian Renaissance poet Ariosto about a small house being perfectly adequate, fitted with an iron gate that opens to an expanse of lawn beyond. Revitalizing this garden was such an opportunity to work in tandem with like-minded clients. The house and garden are now owned by a new family who looked specifically to buy a Shaw house and garden. They picked a beauty!

May in the Sunken Garden with *Geranium x magnificum*, vigorous *Phlox paniculata* 'Laura', and *Stachys* 'Helen von Stein'.

The central bed now features *Iris sibirica* 'Caesar's Brother', *Nepeta fassenii* 'Blue Wonder' and *Geranium x magnificum*, replacing a carpet of *Euonymus colorartus* that was in place when we started the project.

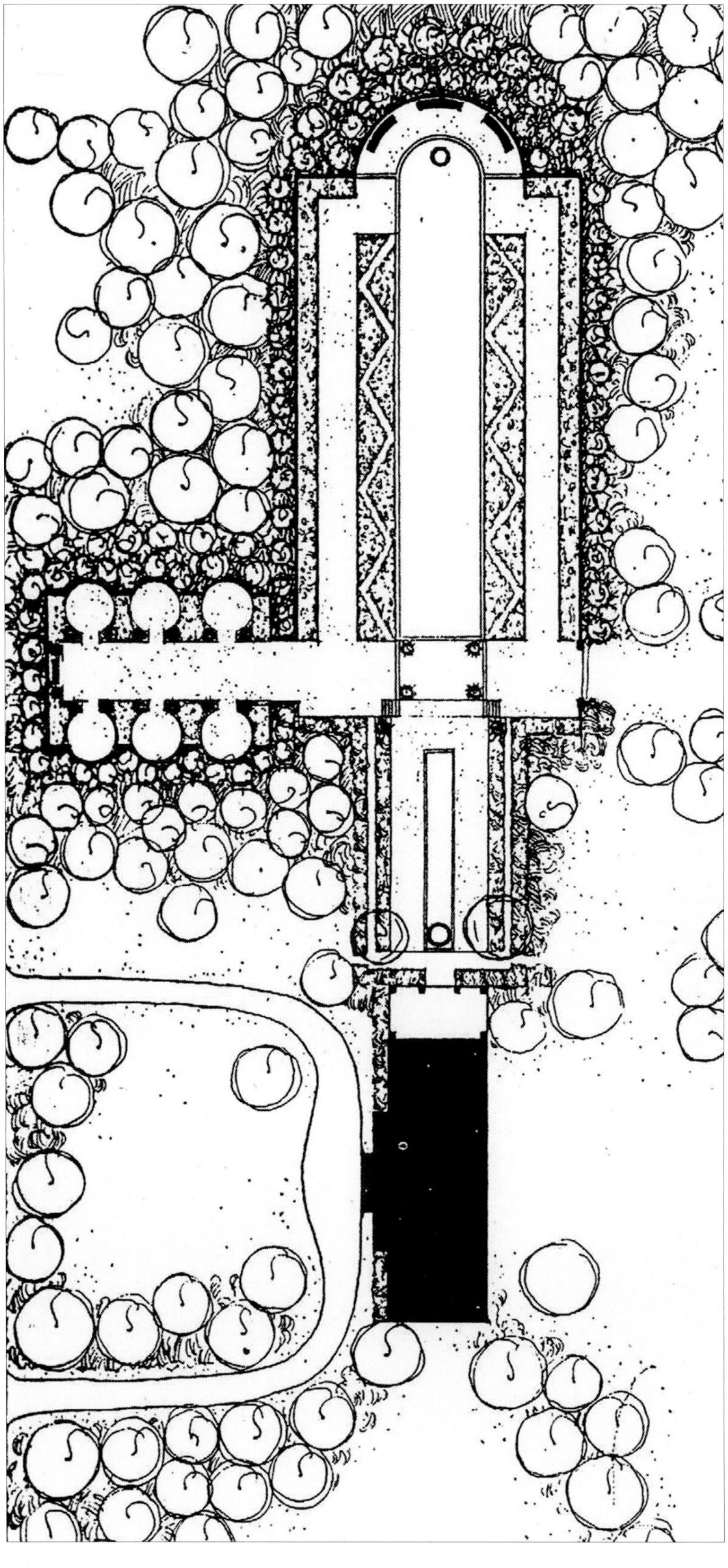

Designed by CB & CF
BUXUS HEDGE W/ WAVE PROFILE
1/8" = 1'-0"
SCULPTED CORNUS MAS HEDGE
1/8" = 1'-0"
North
Scale: 1/8" = 1'-0"
Please Note: This is not a construction drawing.

Original plan (above) and CBLD plan; Howard Van Doren Shaw's garden inspiration from the *Generalife* garden at the Alhambra is apparent with central water and masonry detailing. The later Stroll Garden is on the left.

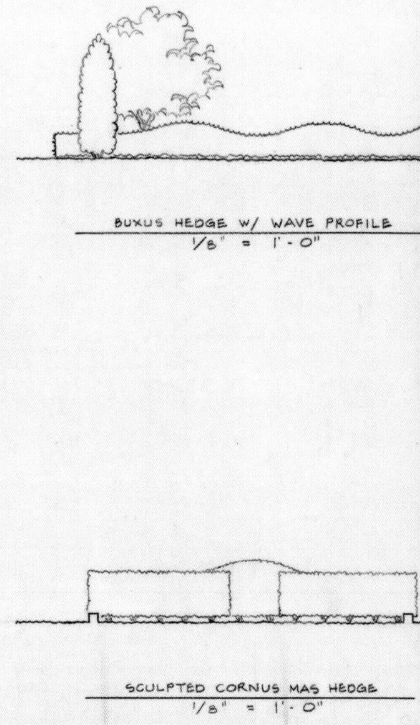

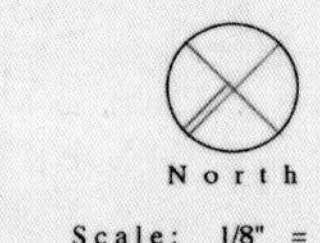

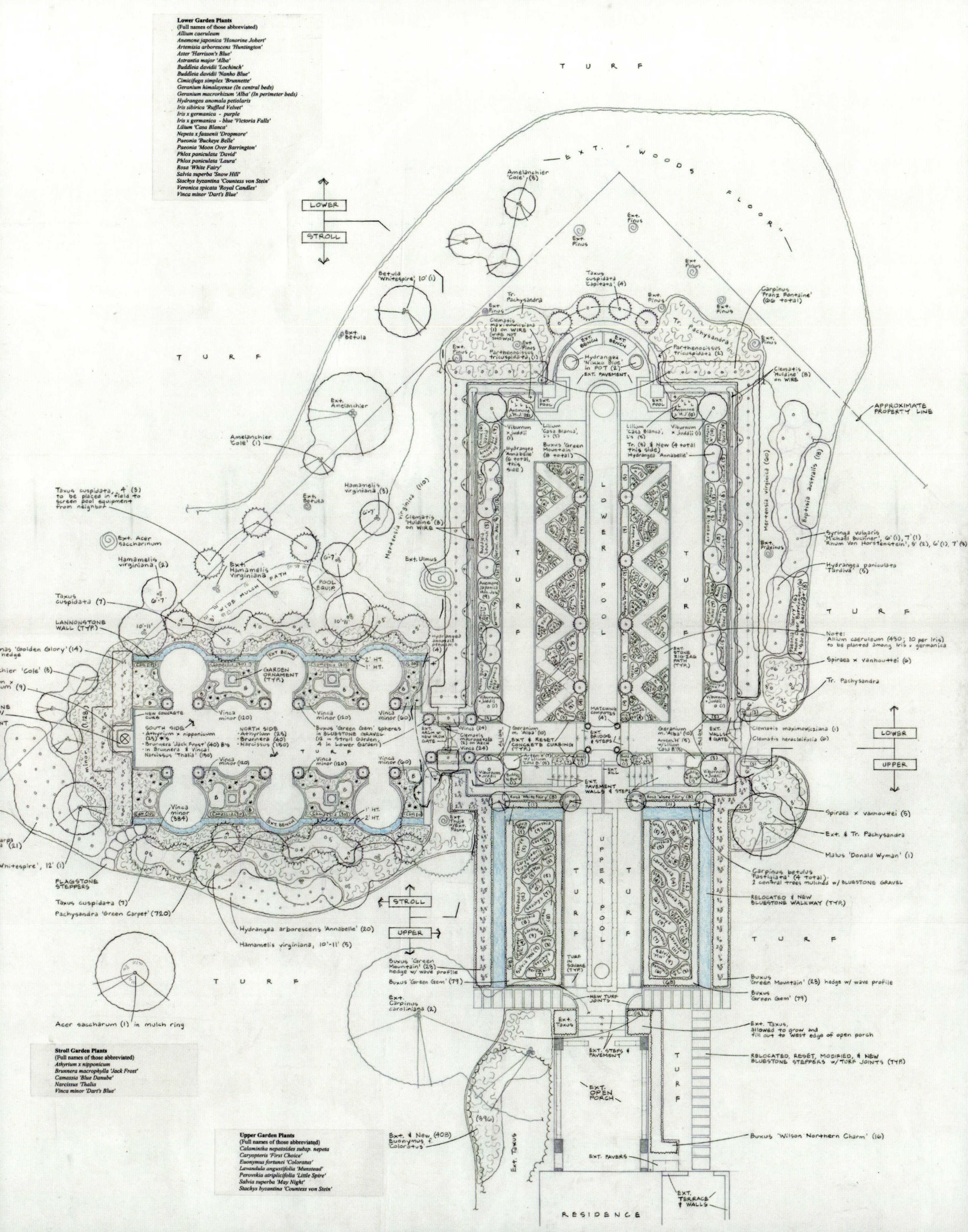
Lower Garden Plants
(Full names of those abbreviated)
Allium caeruleum
Anemone japonica 'Honorine Jobert'
Artemisia arborescens 'Huntington'
Aster 'Harrison's Blue'
Astrantia major 'Alba'
Buddleia davidii 'Lochinch'
Buddleia davidii 'Nanho Blue'
Cimicifuga simplex 'Brunnette'
Geranium himalayense (In central beds)
Geranium macrorhizum 'Alba' (In perimeter beds)
Hydrangea anomala petiolaris
Iris sibirica 'Ruffled Velvet'
Iris x germanica - purple
Iris x germanica - blue 'Victoria Falls'
Lilium 'Casa Blanca'
Nepeta x faassenii 'Dropmore'
Paeonia 'Buckeye Belle'
Paeonia 'Moon Over Barrington'
Phlox paniculata 'David'
Phlox paniculata 'Laura'
Rosa 'White Fairy'
Salvia superba 'Snow Hill'
Stachys byzantina 'Countess von Stein'
Veronica spicata 'Royal Candles'
Vinca minor 'Dart's Blue'
TURF
EXT. "WOODS FLOOR"
LOWER
STROLL
Amelanchier 'Cole' (5)
Ext. Pinus
Betula 'Whitespire', 10' (1)
Ext. Betula
Taxus cuspidata 'Capitata' (4)
Tr. Pachysandra
Carpinus 'Franz Fontaine' (66 total)
Clematis maximowicziana (1) on WIRE (WIRE NOT SHOWN)
Parthenocissus tricuspidata (1)
Hydrangea 'Nikko Blue' in POT (2)
EXT. PAVEMENT
EXT. BENCH
EXT. POOL
Parthenocissus tricuspidata (2)
Clematis 'Huldine' (8) on WIRE
APPROXIMATE PROPERTY LINE
Ext. Amelanchier
Amelanchier 'Cole' (1)
Viburnum x juddii (1)
Lilium 'Casa Blanca'
Hydrangea 'Annabelle' (6 total, this side)
Buxus 'Green Mountain'
Tr. (6) & New (4 total this side)
Hydrangea 'Annabelle'
Baptisia australis (18)
Mertensia virginica (110)
Mertensia virginica (90)
Taxus cuspidata, 4' (3) to be placed in field to screen pool equipment from neighbor
Ext. Betula
Hamamelis virginiana (3)
Clematis 'Huldine' (8) on WIRE
LOWER POOL
TURF
Syringa vulgaris 'Michael Buchner', 6' (1), 7' (1)
'Rhum Von Horstenstein', 5' (2), 6' (1), 7' (4)
Ext. Fraxinus
Ext. Acer saccharinum
Hamamelis virginiana (2)
Ext. Hamamelis virginiana
WIDE MULCH PATH
POOL EQUIP.
Ext. Ulmus
Hydrangea paniculata 'Tardiva' (5)
Taxus cuspidata (7)
LANNONSTONE WALL (TYP.)
TURF
Note: Allium caeruleum (430; 10 per Iris) to be planted among Iris x germanica
EXT. STONE ZIG-ZAG PATH (TYP.)
Spiraea x vanhouttei (6)
Tr. Pachysandra
EXT. BENCH
2' HT.
1' HT.
GARDEN ORNAMENT (TYP.)
NEW CONCRETE CURB
SOUTH SIDE
• Athyrium x nipponicum (25) 8"s
• Brunnera 'Jack Frost' (40) 8"s in Brunnera & Vinca
• Narcissus 'Thalia' (150)
NORTH SIDE
• Athyrium (25)
• Brunnera (40)
• Narcissus (150)
Vinca minor (120)
Vinca minor (60)
Buxus 'Green Gem' spheres in BLUESTONE GRAVEL (12 in Stroll Garden, 4 in Lower Garden)
Vinca (24)
Geranium m. 'Alba' (20)
EXT. & RESET CONCRETE CURBING (TYP.)
MATCHING CONCRETE (4)
EXT. BRIDGE & STEPS
Clematis maximowicziana (1)
Clematis heracleifolia (6)
LOWER
UPPER
Vinca minor (384)
EXT. PAVEMENT WALLS & STEPS
Rosa 'White Fairy' (8)
Spiraea x vanhouttei (5)
Ext. & Tr. Pachysandra
Malus 'Donald Wyman' (1)
Betula 'Whitespire', 12' (1)
FLAGSTONE STEPPERS
Taxus cuspidata (7)
Pachysandra 'Green Carpet' (720)
UPPER POOL
TURF
Carpinus betulus 'Fastigiata' (4 total), 2 central trees mulched w/ BLUESTONE GRAVEL
RELOCATED & NEW BLUESTONE WALKWAY (TYP.)
STROLL
UPPER
Hydrangea arborescens 'Annabelle' (20)
Hamamelis virginiana, 10'-11' (5)
TURF
TURF
Buxus 'Green Mountain' (23) hedge w/ wave profile
Buxus 'Green Gem' (79)
TURF IN SQUARE (TYP.)
Buxus 'Green Mountain' (23) hedge w/ wave profile
Buxus 'Green Gem' (79)
Ext. Carpinus caroliniana (2)
NEW TURF JOINTS
Ext. Taxus
Ext. Taxus, allowed to grow and fill out to west edge of open porch
Acer saccharum (1) in mulch ring
EXT. STEPS & PAVEMENT
RELOCATED, RESET, MODIFIED, & NEW BLUESTONE STEPPERS w/ TURF JOINTS (TYP.)
TURF
EXT. OPEN PORCH
Stroll Garden Plants
(Full names of those abbreviated)
Athyrium x nipponicum
Brunnera macrophylla 'Jack Frost'
Camassia 'Blue Danube'
Narcissus 'Thalia'
Vinca minor 'Dart's Blue'
Ext. & New (408) Euonymus f. 'Coloratus'
(396)
Ext. Taxus
Buxus 'Wilson Northern Charm' (16)
EXT. PAVERS
EXT. TERRACE & WALLS
Upper Garden Plants
(Full names of those abbreviated)
Calamintha nepetoides subsp. nepeta
Caryopteris 'First Choice'
Euonymus fortunei 'Coloratus'
Lavandula angustifolia 'Munstead'
Perovskia atriplicifolia 'Little Spire'
Salvia superba 'May Night'
Stachys byzantina 'Countess von Stein'
RESIDENCE

Above: The fieldstone wall at the edge of the drive creates an intimate entry experience.

Opposite, top: Boxwood replaces juniper spires along the edge of the rill, a change that reflects the current light and moisture conditions. ***Opposite, bottom:*** A bronze figure of a potter by an unknown artist is installed in the Stroll Garden.

Top: A raised stone basin at the end of the rill is accentuated by bold potted *Hydrangea macrophylla* 'Bailmer'. ***Bottom left:*** The upper rill planting beds contain full-sun loving, deer-resistant herbaceous perennials, including *Perovskia x* 'Longhin' and *Calamintha x* 'White Cloud' framed by wave box hedges.

Right: A heraldic gateway signals the entrance to the west meadow. The adjoining hedge of *Carpinus betulus* 'Frans Fontaine' creates the walled enclosure.

PARVA·SED·APT
OBNOXIA·SED
PARTA·MEO·SED
IHI·SED·NV
NON·SORDIDA
EN·AERE·DOM

Asian Influence

These clients were hoping to create a garden inspired by Chinese art, one that would blend well with Illinois nature. East meets West in the best sense. A first visit to this large, wooded property revealed a house the client proclaimed to be a "Rube Goldberg machine" due to uncoordinated building additions and expansions that had all been attached to the small home over decades. The owners are avid collectors of antiques including regional American maps, early European globes, and ancient Asian sculptures, so they could recognize with proportion-and-design-honed eyes that the site needed help from professionals.

Expanding upon the owners' interests, we suggested a series of island beds conceived to reference their ancient maps—continents of plantings in a sea of lawn, if you will. As the garden expanded, we did significant research to nestle their other collection, the Chinese sculptures, into plants of Chinese provenance to give context and an extra layer of meaning. Of course, the site is in Illinois; we mixed in some native plants and ensured that Chinese plants had not been identified as invasive species that could harm the native woodland adjacent.

Nothing is more tasty to deer than exotic plants, so before any of the garden was built, we fenced in the area closest to the house. Several years later, we enclosed the entire twelve-acre property with New Zealand woven wire elk fencing—strong enough to keep the deer out and durable enough to survive the occasional falling branch. Amazingly, the first spring after the big corral was erected, the woodland floor was carpeted with *Trillium grandiflora*. The owners had never seen such abundance in the thirty years since they purchased the property.

The clients own an international manufacturing business with factories around the world, which allows them to collect art widely. There was so much shoved haphazardly into an old pole barn on site that we urged the owners to build a museum. Years later, they hired an architect friend, Laurence (Larry) Booth, to construct one; today the gallery has a full-time curator and is visited by scholars from around the globe. We helped them to choose white oak-gray for this new building to connect it to the woodland and suggested visually linking it to the motor court paving with a stone walkway of shipping-ballast Chinese sandstone.

Sixteenth-century bronze temple bells throughout the garden are mounted on wooden supports we designed.

The Gallery Garden's covered walkway approach is screened from the main house by an underplanting of native oaks and hickories. An open gravel court from southwest leads to an open lawn used for receptions and provides a clearing that accentuates by contrast the density of the woods beyond. A Chinese pagoda as ornament provides scale to the mature trees and twenty-foot-tall winged columns in the distance. Two-ton granite Buddhas were placed at the edge of the woods (looking east or southeast, as is tradition) by an innovative piece of equipment with major balloon-like inflated tires on an articulated tractor; installation was scheduled in the depths of most-frozen winter to avoid root compression.

The garden, like the owner's business, continued to expand over thirty-five years, so finding plants that could more or less manage themselves was paramount. A key tactic was using a pleasant repetition of plant varieties that were successful—without making it look like we had taken advantage of an end-of-season sale on any one plant—and achieved this by placing them so they would reveal their presence gradually as a visitor moves through the garden. Incorporating drifts of plants also allows us to divide and replant elsewhere in new beds. "Shopping at home" is a great way of economizing.

Whenever the owners returned from a trip to the Far East, they would tell us about a new piece of art or sculpture they had purchased and was soon to be delivered, allowing us to start thinking about how to incorporate it even before its arrival. The strategic placement of ancient figures and bells certainly sets an Asian mood, but so does the collection of containers. Two-hundred year-old iron, Vietnamese clay, and unique pots were periodically brought in with shipments of museum acquisitions—these quickly grew to number over fifty. We ultimately resolved the challenge of organizing massive, sometimes forty-inch-diameter diameter pots into the garden by planting them with just one or two species, thus taking advantage of the scale to use plants that normally are not suited to containers—it's easier than maintaining a mixed planter as well. Evergreens and specimen woody plants that are left all year proved to be helpful and multi-season options.

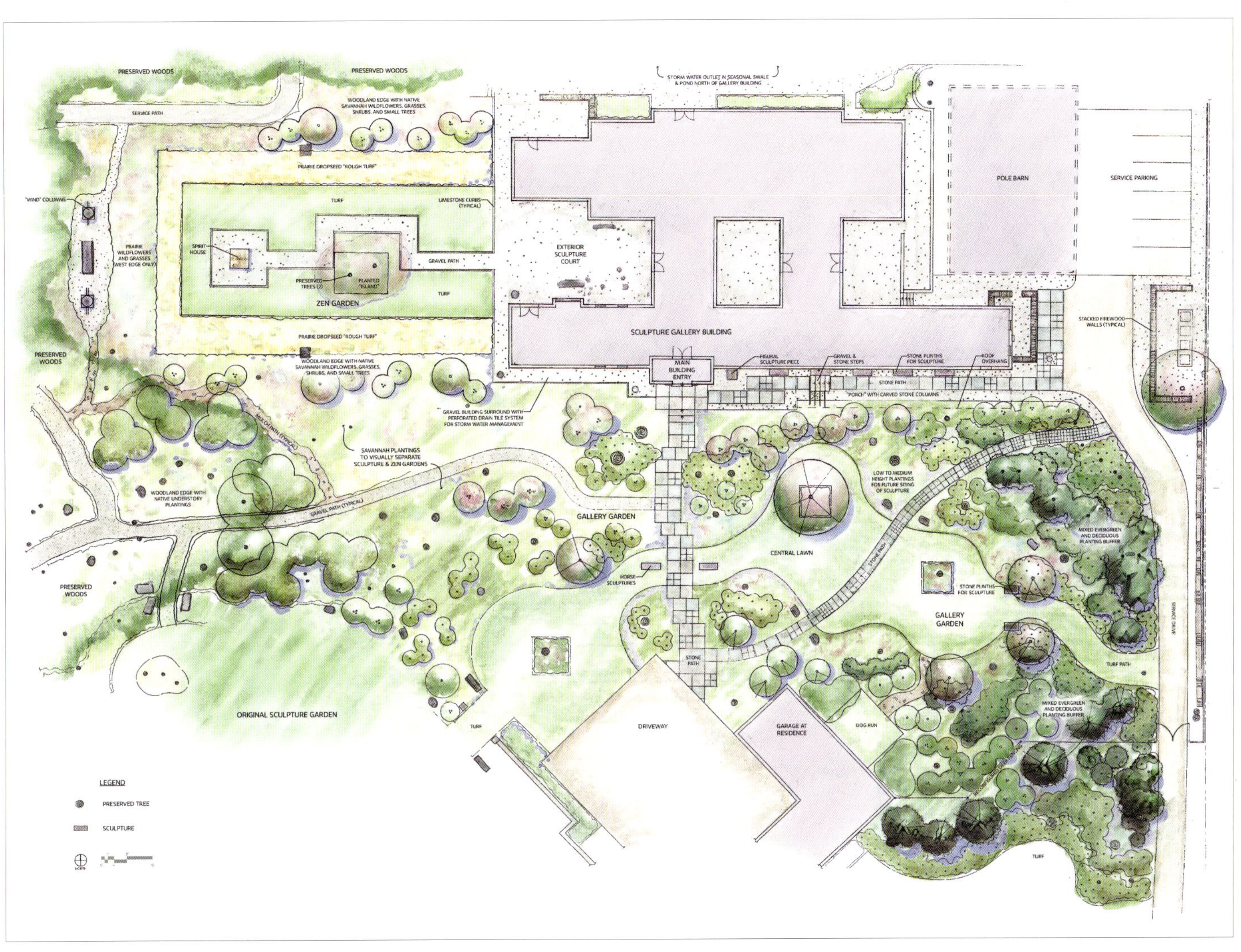

Opposite, top: A life-size granite horse, Qing Dynasty, in the winter garden. ***Opposite, bottom left:*** Herbaceous Asiatic garden plants surround nineteenth-century stone figures of Chinese officials in the island beds.

Opposite, bottom right: A seventeenth-century Fu lion on the pool terrace with *Fallopia japonica* 'Variegata'. ***Above:*** Gallery entry garden plan.

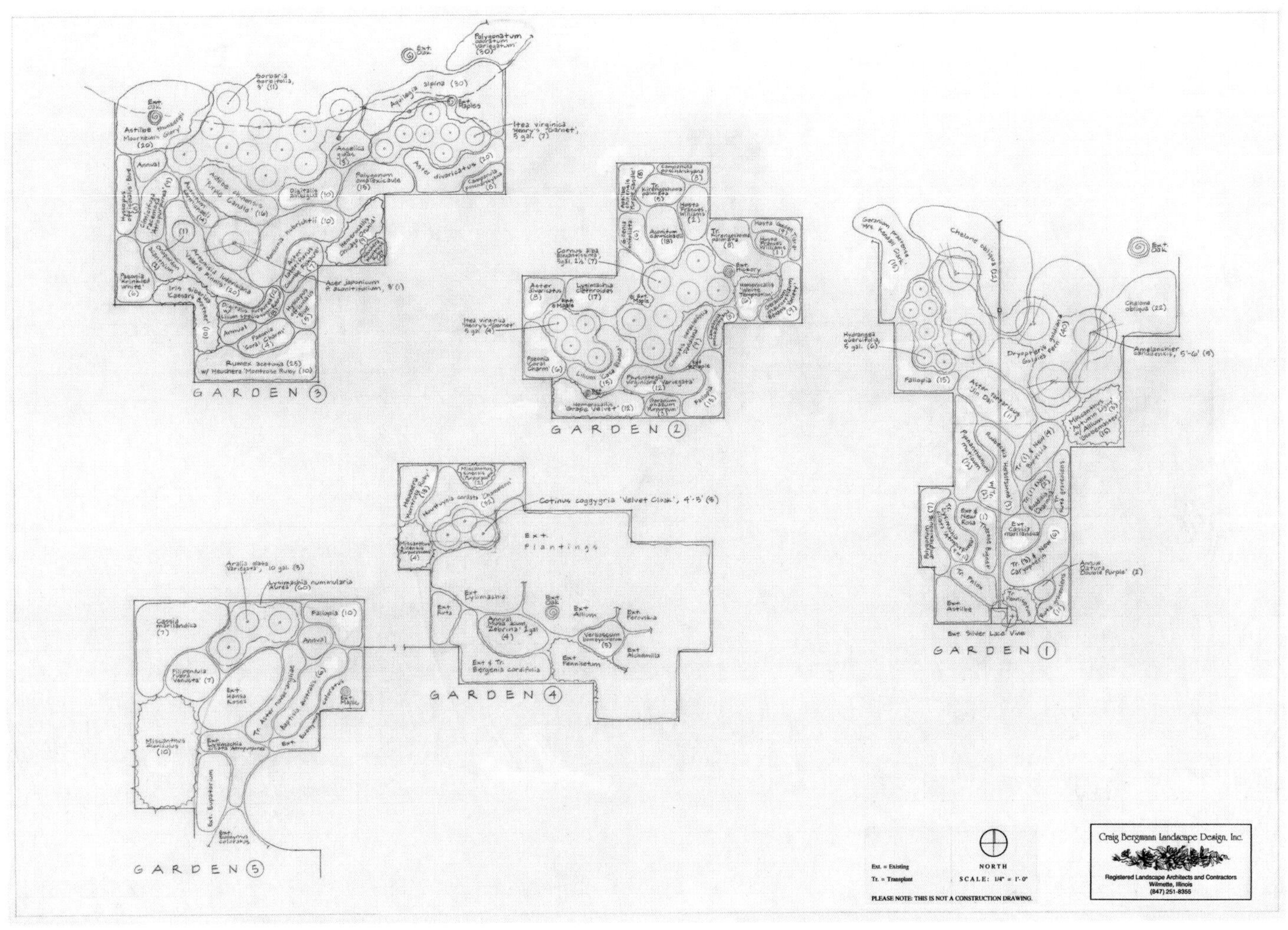

Opposite: An early twentieth-century Thai teak ceiling panel reconceived as a garden gate. *Above:* Island bed planting plan.

Overleaf: Granite Buddhas are installed at the edge of the woods amid *Hydrangea* 'Limelight' and *Hosta* 'Royal Standard'.

Top: Sculpture on the gallery path with the native *Acer saccharum*. *Above:* An ancient cast-iron vessel with *Ensente ventricosum* 'Maurelli' and *Stephanandra incisa* 'Crispa' in full flower.

Right: Chinese pagoda at the end of the Zen-inspired path.

Adding Personality

For us, adding ornament to a garden is much like accessorizing an outfit with jewelry or putting the finishing decorative touches on a beautiful room. Due to the Midwestern climate, we must be very careful about storing precious patinated objects through the winter to ensure survival. Often we use vintage or reproduction containers and objects simply because they are more durable and affordable. We mix the occasional antique with the new to add a sense of history to a newly created space—this also translates to many as sophistication. We often continue to add ornamentation to a garden, bit by bit, for years after the initial installation as we happen across just the right piece or a welcome addition to a collection. It's easy to over-ornament a space, so we find we have to restrain ourselves. We review gardens seasonally so that they don't end up looking cluttered—that diverts attention away from the main design intent. Craig tends to take on most of this detail work because he's an avid collector himself and will readily admit he simply loves to shop, often buying pieces without an end placement in mind, but always telling himself and anyone else who asks that he'll find a place for it in a client's garden . . .

An American terra-cotta urn, 1940s, with a terra-cotta apple, a stone finial, 1920s, and a reproduction strap-metal bench all set on a random-stone patio with planted joints.

Naturalistic Gardens

Geum triflorum graces the spring woodland floor.

When a client requests a nature-inspired landscape, our first conversation is often centered around defining "natural." It's a term open to broad interpretation. We believe that first looking at any site honestly to assess its existing positives, as well as its limitations, will guide us in selecting the right plants for the place, to create an aesthetic that feels more as if it were designed by Mother Nature than our hand, which we find is usually what clients are after.

In other words, we allow the directive in creating naturalistic gardens to originate with the unique attributes of the existing site as much as from a collaboration with the client. Our interpretation from inspirational natural areas often drives our composition of plants, in a way that we hope is an artful emulation. By contrast with more controlled, imposed landscape solutions that have the creation of a specific theme or style as a goal, a change of existing site conditions is often the prerequisite. In following a natural approach, the most important choice often lies with a predominant use of less-cultivated plant varieties. Subtle foliage contrasts, less emphasis on constant color, and repeated natural forms are major factors in achieving success for these gardens. As they develop, we've also found that interpretive editing of the plant collection is required to emulate the way plant colonies naturally spread and communicate. This allows for personalization of preferences—ours as well as the owners'—and keeps our relationships current.

Often a naturally styled garden is a mix of native plants and cultivars arranged with contrasting masses of natural-appearing plants—designed with intention but not obvious at first glance—instead of emulating nature's outright serendipitous organization. Either approach works, which route to take just needs to be defined and explained along the way.

We are so pleased that there is an increased awareness surrounding native species today. After years of feeling as though we needed to convince clients to use them, we finally feel we can now speak a common language with many homeowners. Our practice has always started with natives, or their cultivars, in our plant selections because of the reality that plants already growing in a region are simply going to be hardier than those imported. What we've learned over the years is that if natives are used in a cultivated growing environment, the plants will grow distinctly differently than they would in the wild, or even die, if tended too much. When left on their own, natives—and especially prairie species—develop mechanisms to survive, such as deep roots, drought tolerance, and inherent chemical defenses from pests. Planting them in garden-mix soil and offering supplemental irrigation can lead to shallow roots, floppy, excessively tall foliage, and diluted internal chemical defenses. Such plants will not thrive or will be eaten by insects or rabbits and deer. One important and prevalent misunderstanding we work to correct in our interview process with clients is the idea that natural gardening requires less maintenance. Naturalistic gardens simply require different maintenance from conventional gardens and different levels of intervention.

The golden rule for a creating a true native garden setting using native plants means using native soil profiles, water levels, exposure, and sunlight. If creating a naturalistic garden from a clean slate or compromised site, search for native soil to import, not from a topsoil broker, but from nearby construction sites. Save site-fallen leaves and shred them for nutritious soil-building mulch to use in naturalized woodland areas. Cut back spent foliage only later in the spring so the beneficial insect populations, which often lay eggs in the stems of herbaceous plants the previous growing season, have shelter to survive the winter and procreate. To create a truly splendid naturalistic garden, you must also enter into a pact with Nature to honor and support her time-honored processes, which are quite obvious, if we just take the time to listen and observe.

Where Prairie Meets Dune

This property on a bluff overlooking Lake Michigan originally belonged to the client's father, and it had long held a simple ranch-style house. When the client and his wife decided to replace it with their dream home, they wanted to reference the region's historical Prairie Style architecture and to create an appropriately complementary landscape. Architect Scott Fortman was called into action and referred Craig and Donald Bolak to partner on the site development and landscaping—all before the demolition of the original house. This gave us some great opportunities to make a plan for protecting mature trees outside of the new house's footprint, use the old driveway for construction access, and to install proactive systems for managing storm water, all elements that helped set up the new construction for success and settle into the neighborhood from day one.

The specific goal for the garden was to create a small wildlife "island" on this suburban bluff, an oasis for birds and pollinators set amid highly cultivated properties all around. Our directive for plant selection was to choose native plantings for shade and sun areas wherever possible, to follow strictly sustainable processes during the building of the new landscape, and to plan for organic maintenance to follow. Familiar native perennials incorporated include wild ginger, sedges, wild geranium, shooting stars, bee balms, butterfly weeds, coneflowers, switch-grass, multiple dune grasses, and the showy native hibiscus of the wet prairie. Sumacs, serviceberries, birch and white pine are included in the woody plant palette.

Fortunately, we have worked on several original Frank Lloyd Wright sites in our area; these historical landscapes taught us how to interpret the aesthetic intention of the style with plants. The shady front garden contains a few period-appropriate cultivated species to provide a bit of evergreen structure in the landscape for the winter months, but we did add prairie plants we found in archival photos of properties on neighboring sites as well. Three containers integrated into the architecture of the entrance court feature some of the same natives as the main garden, with a focus on colorful blooming plants.

A naturalistic-style planting based on curved forms in the larger backyard areas acts as a foil to the architecture's angular geometry. The practice of not removing fallen branches or much of the natural leaf litter from the trees is quickly reestablishing some of the original woodland here, another of the client's goals. If leaf accumulation occurs too heavily in some areas, it is relocated as mulch to cover an area with exposed soil.

We set a true rain garden at the lowest point on the property. In a major rain event and during spring thaw, as the area pools in the central planting bed to depth of eight inches, an overflow drain collects the excess water and flows it under the dune to percolate slowly into the beach sand beyond. The marginal aquatic selection of native plants includes switch grasses, Joe Pye weeds of various scale, composites, swamp hibiscus, and multiple species of lobelias that thrive and reseed with abandon.

Saving the Bur oak that stood in the center of the old circle driveway has been quite the "assisted living" approach to arboriculture. As we all know, the older things become, the less receptive they are to change. To prep the tree for disruption during construction, we root pruned it to give critical roots time to reestablish during the two-year project, canopy pruned it to reduce the amount of energy it would need to expend to keep itself alive during construction, used time-release organic fertilizer to stimulate new root growth and strong foliage, amended the soil with mycorrhizae to optimize available nutrients during a time of stress, and watered it during hot weather months to ensure it didn't struggle to stay hydrated. We are waiting patiently to see if our efforts made a difference in its survival, and it is working so far.

Front woodland approach with preserved *Pinus strobus* and naturalized *Carex pennsylvanica*.

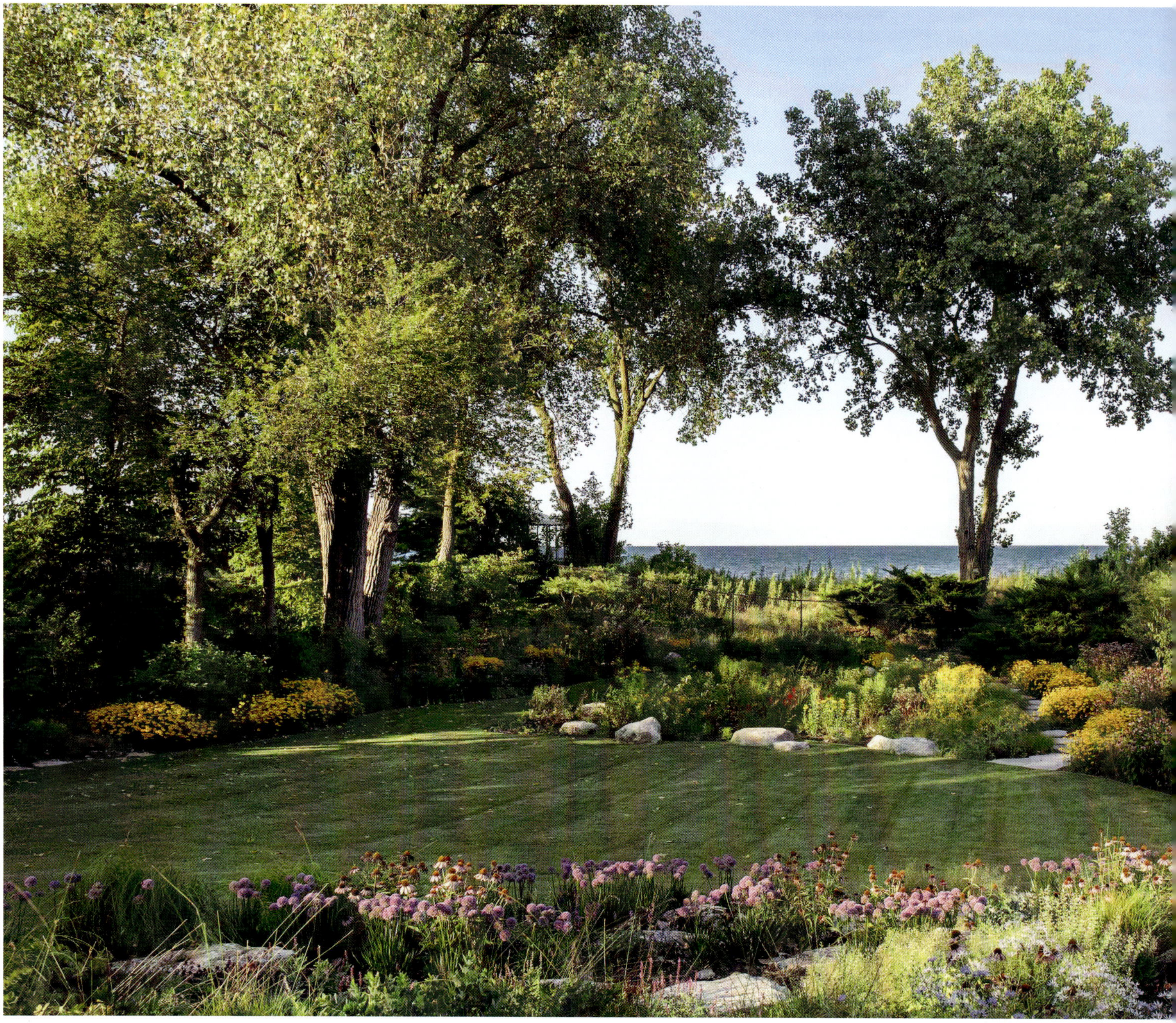

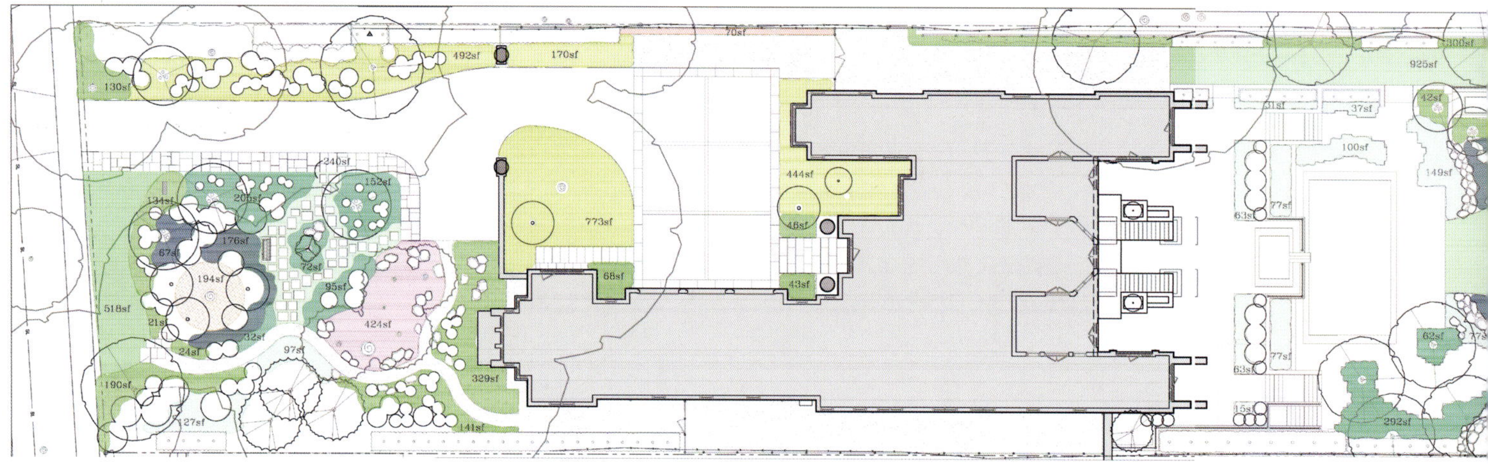

70sf
492sf
170sf
130sf
240sf
152sf
134sf
205sf
176sf
67sf
72sf
773sf
194sf
95sf
68sf
518sf
21sf
424sf
32sf
24sf
97sf
329sf
190sf
127sf
141sf
444sf
46sf
43sf
300sf
925sf
42sf
31sf
37sf
100sf
149sf
77sf
63sf
62sf
77sf
63sf
15sf
292sf

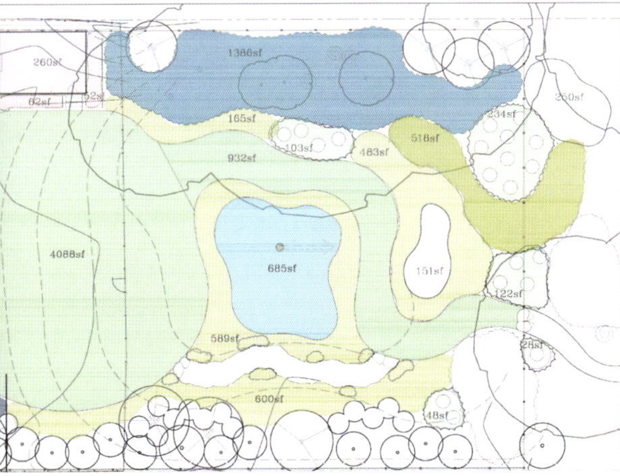

Top left: Pool terrace promontory with a view across the rock garden, the central rain garden, and the dunes to Lake Michigan beyond. ***Bottom left:*** Schematic landscape plan. ***Above:*** *Narcissus poeticus* and *Cercis canadensis* in bloom close to the house.

Above: An intimate dining space on the pool terrace. *Opposite:* View across the garden from the house to the lake.

Overleaf: The challenging site demanded a terraced, cultivated experience with the use of native plant species whenever possible.

Nature as Therapy

Decades ago, we were called upon to help enhance a property with a woodland that cascaded down from a bluff and into a ravine. There was not a scrap of lawn on the property—the kind of thing that excited us and let us know immediately that the clients, pediatric specialists, were kindred spirits on the first visit Cathrine Dammann and Craig paid—they clearly loved the property for what it was and didn't want to change it dramatically. The house had been built in the 1920s by a local architect for his own family, so the attention to the siting and reverence for its dramatic contours was palpable. With nature already taking a strong hand here, the project told us very clearly to "tread lightly." We took time to ensure we understood the ecosystem we were working in and to document the existing plant population so that we could honor and enhance it.

Still, any property that has endured for nearly a century needs updates. The driveway surface was badly in need of repair, so we looked on this as an opportunity to tell a story by creating a new drive. Instead of bordering the asphalt with decorative premade paver details in a conventional way, we decided to create asymmetric patterns set just below the topmost asphalt surface of the drive, so it looked as if there was an old street paved in brick peeking through. We chose local flagstone to complement this and to create an organic, meandering walk approach to each of the home's several entry doors. The remaining planting spaces are filled with casual tumblers and traditional cottage-style plants, fulfilling the owners' wishes for a flowery approach that also ended up being easier to care for than the wildly prolific woodland. We nestled the house into its sunny setting, surrounding it with a frame of native sumacs and serviceberries for summertime appreciation.

An informal "archaeological process" revealed fascinating elements from the original patio. The previous owners had collected stones every time they took a walk on the beach, just a block away. We found these regularly while planting the space surrounding the hand-chiseled square flagstone patio fitted with a central cast-stone basin. We re-told their story by assembling the excavated stones to form the edging of the existing path system. The spring revealed dense carpets of *Scilla siberica* and *Eranthus hyemalis* that dies back in the summer. These are non-natives, but still wonderful signifiers of a glorious period in the gardening year. A hollowed-out stump was repurposed as a container, and other mossy old clay pots are strategically placed to give just a hint of seasonal color.

The seasons are nowhere more apparent than in the woodland full of ephemerals. Dramatic and ever-changing angles of sun highlight different surfaces and places throughout the year. We propped up ancient witch hazel shrub trunks with forked branches to reveal a space underneath for a child's sitting area and a ring of stumps, à la Jens Jensen. Much to our surprise, during the first fall after we started work on the property and the leaf canopy dissipated, we could see that there was an actual Jensen stone counsel ring across the ravine on the neighboring property, enjoying the same view from a different angle—kismet! This space quickly became a vital patient-doctor therapy room for the child psychologist owner.

Preserving woodlands also means embracing the full cycle of tree life; as trees gradually died and were removed before they could threaten the terra-cotta tile roof of the house, we cut the trunks into uniform lengths and stacked them into a serpentine pile to create a unique stack of firewood, as well as to provide year-round screening of the neighboring property's driveway. As the logs started to decay, the owners decided not to burn any more of them, but to let the pile become a habitat for the local chipmunks and beneficial insects.

Our original clients eventually had to move away; they took time to search out a new owner who would love this place as they did, however. The home is now owned by a local architect friend who has breathed much-needed care into the systems and structure of the house to ensure that this lovely place will last another hundred years. We are fortunate as well to be helping the current owner with her landscape needs as they reveal themselves in this ever-changing woodland.

Native woodland in spring with naturalized Narcissus.

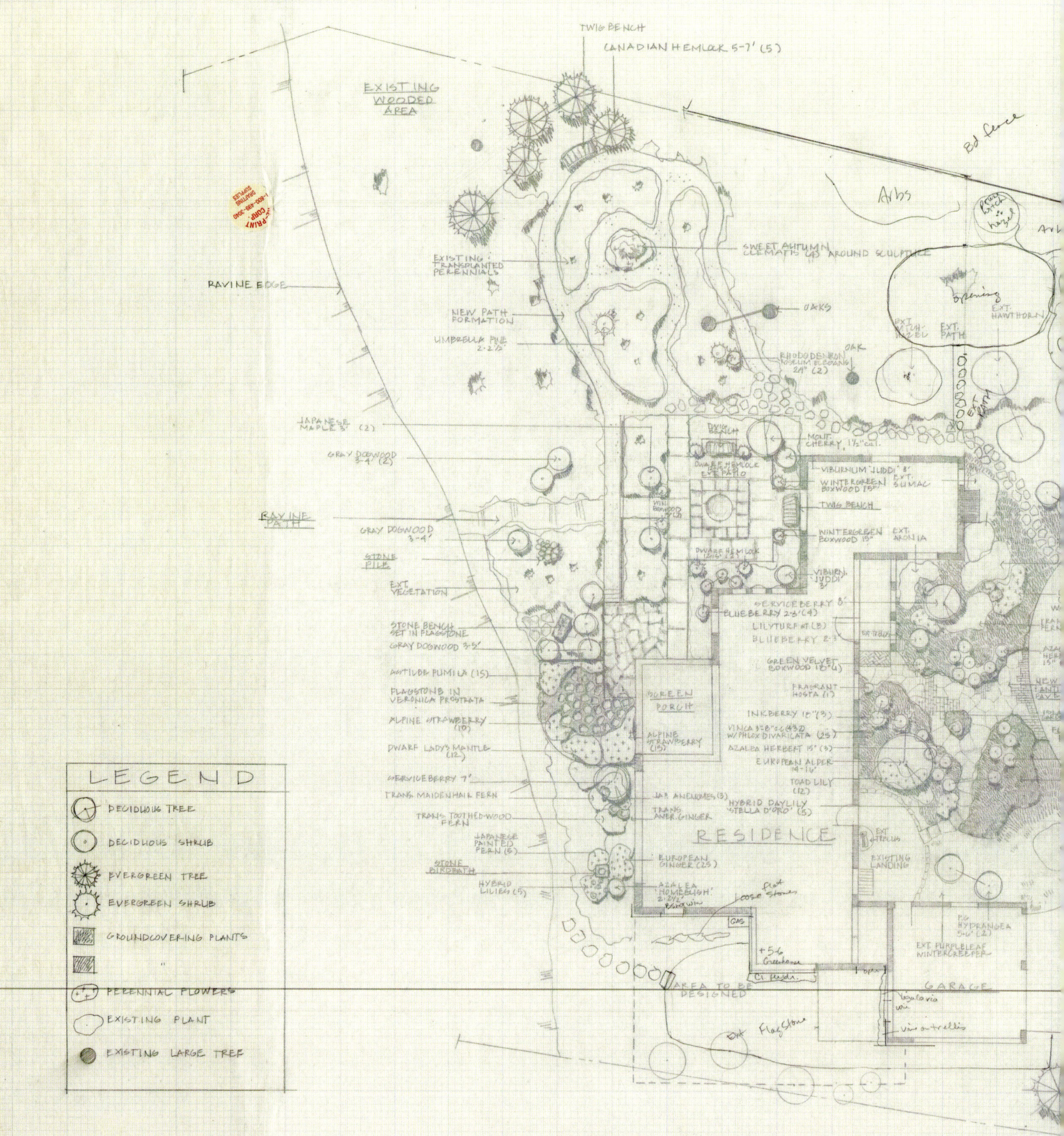

TWIG BENCH
CANADIAN HEMLOCK 5-7' (5)
EXISTING WOODED AREA
RAVINE EDGE
EXISTING TRANSPLANTED PERENNIALS
SWEET AUTUMN CLEMATIS (4) AROUND SCULPTURE
NEW PATH FORMATION
OAKS
UMBRELLA PINE 2-2½'
OAK
JAPANESE MAPLE 3' (2)
GRAY DOGWOOD 3-4' (2)
MONT. CHERRY 1½" cal.
VIBURNUM 'JUDDI' 8'
WINTERGREEN BOXWOOD 15"
EXT. SUMAC
TWIG BENCH
RAVINE PATH
GRAY DOGWOOD 3-4'
STONE PILE
WINTERGREEN BOXWOOD 15"
EXT. ARONIA
EXT. VEGETATION
SERVICEBERRY 8'
BLUEBERRY 2-3' (4)
LILYTURF (8)
BLUEBERRY 2-3'
STONE BENCH SET IN FLAGSTONE
GRAY DOGWOOD 3-5'
ASTILBE PUMILA (15)
GREEN VELVET BOXWOOD (8"-4)
FRAGRANT HOSTA (1)
FLAGSTONE IN VERONICA PROSTRATA
SCREEN PORCH
INKBERRY 18" (3)
ALPINE STRAWBERRY (10)
ALPINE STRAWBERRY (15)
DWARF LADY'S MANTLE (12)
AZALEA HERBERT 15" (4)
EUROPEAN ALDER 14-16'
SERVICEBERRY 7'
TOAD LILY (12)
TRANS. MAIDENHAIR FERN
HYBRID DAYLILY 'STELLA D'ORO' (5)
TRANS. TOOTHED WOOD FERN
TRANS. ANEM. GINGER
RESIDENCE
JAPANESE PAINTED FERN (5)
EXISTING LANDING
EUROPEAN GINGER (25)
STONE BIRDBATH
HYBRID LILIES (5)
EXT. PURPLELEAF WINTERCREEPER
AREA TO BE DESIGNED
GARAGE
LEGEND
DECIDUOUS TREE
DECIDUOUS SHRUB
EVERGREEN TREE
EVERGREEN SHRUB
GROUNDCOVERING PLANTS
PERENNIAL FLOWERS
EXISTING PLANT
EXISTING LARGE TREE
EXT. HAWTHORN
EXT. PATH

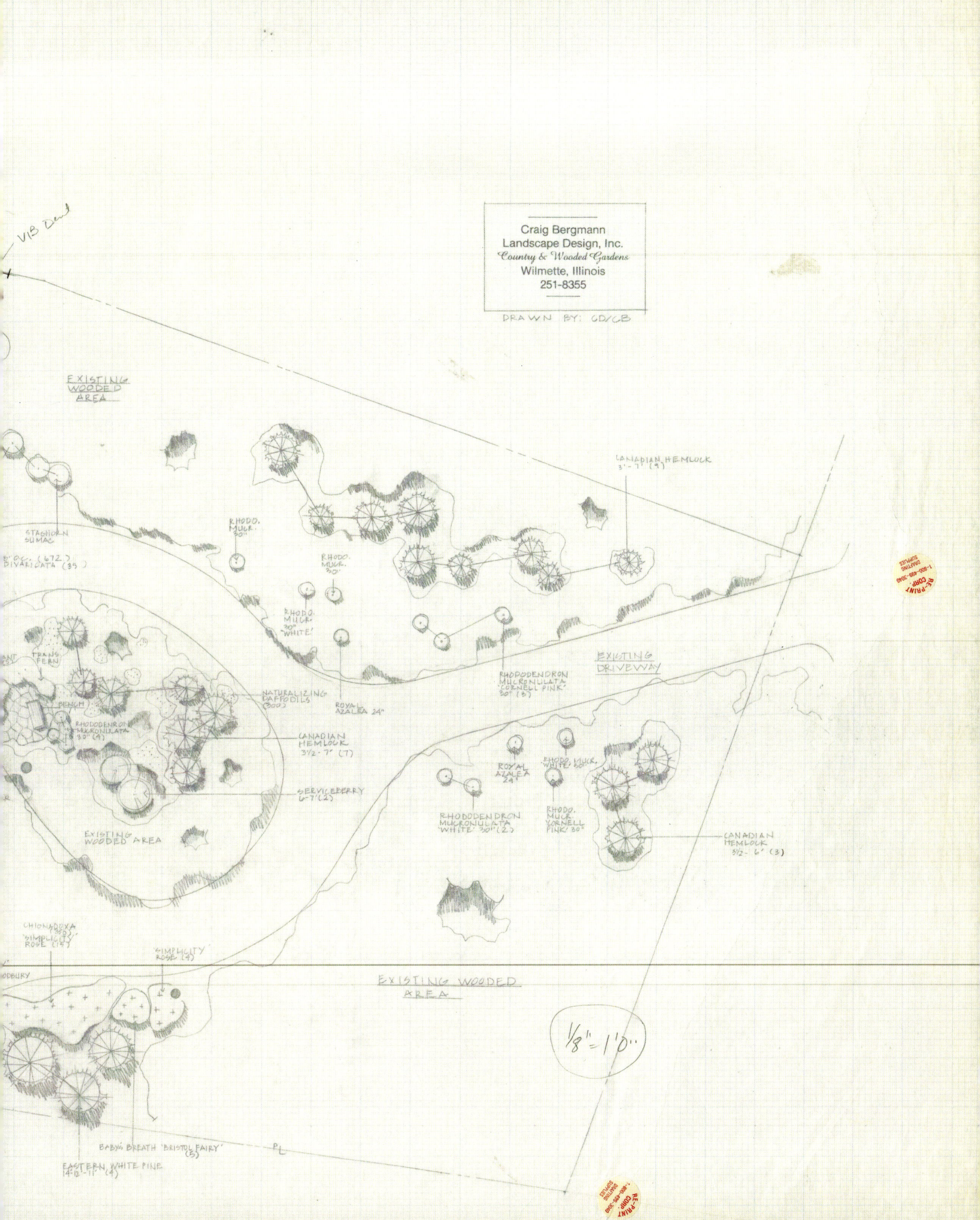

Craig Bergmann
Landscape Design, Inc.
Country & Wooded Gardens
Wilmette, Illinois
251-8355
DRAWN BY: GD/CB
EXISTING WOODED AREA
STAGHORN SUMAC
DIVARICATA (35)
RHODO. MUCR. 30"
RHODO. MUCR. 30"
RHODO. MUCR. 30" 'WHITE'
ROYAL AZALEA 24"
CANADIAN HEMLOCK 3'-7' (9)
RHODODENDRON MUCRONULATA 'CORNELL PINK' 30" (5)
EXISTING DRIVEWAY
TRANS. FERN
BENCH
NATURALIZING DAFFODILS (300)
RHODODENRON MUCRONULATA 30" (4)
CANADIAN HEMLOCK 3½-7' (7)
SERVICEBERRY 6-7' (2)
EXISTING WOODED AREA
ROYAL AZALEA 24"
RHODO. MUCR. 'WHITE' 30"
RHODODENDRON MUCRONULATA 'WHITE' 30" (2)
RHODO. MUCR. 'CORNELL PINK' 30"
CANADIAN HEMLOCK 3½-6' (3)
CHIONADOXA
'SIMPLICITY' ROSE
'SIMPLICITY' ROSE (4)
EXISTING WOODED AREA
1/8" = 1'0"
BABY'S BREATH 'BRISTOL FAIRY' (5)
PL
EASTERN WHITE PINE

Cobbles collected on the property create a natural terracing effect; hand-built twig trellises are affixed to the wall.

The center of the circle drive is an outdoor waiting room for patients and their families.

Ravine Garden

Gardening with a client over many years builds trust and friendship, allowing for boundary-pushing garden design. These clients, Carolyn and Bill, originally lived in a house where we had helped them create a grow-and-show perennial garden along the public sidewalk for the neighborhood to enjoy. Carolyn was a florist at the time, and she wanted her place to be known as "the flower lady's garden."

Fast forward a few years, and they purchased their dream house just a few blocks away. This was a serious property, a turn-of-the-century Dutch colonial set on the edge of a wooded ravine and much more private than their former home. This great old place harkens back to the architectural traditions of the East Coast and even features an entry bridge. As is true for many older homes, the configuration of the rooms was not conducive to today's family lifestyles, so they called in architect Dirk Dennison to add modern conveniences and make it their forever home. This included adding a new garage to the existing structure; they decided to add a modernist note by using earth-toned New York fieldstone and glass, as a contrast to the original clapboard cladding. Its roof provided the perfect perch for a Zen-type hot tub. An old porch was replaced with a casual kid's room set at the edge of the bluff; it was constructed quite close to major oaks, so we insisted on a course of tree protection that saved many of the trees. Craig and Donald Bolak collaborated along the way with the architectural team to design plantings and hardscape that would help the additions blend into the site. On the new garage roof, we filled a planter with dwarf conifers for evergreen interest and to screen the street view. Trees with moderate-height canopies were chosen to surround the house to frame and allow views to the ravine.

For garden spaces on the bluff, the building code restricted the use of subterranean foundations for terraces and walls, so we used large boulders for retention, set on grade in a fashion to make it seem that they had always been there. Bill had requested that we install a "storytelling circle" overlooking the ravine; we chose the same New York fieldstone to keep the palette as consistent and organic as possible. We planted young redbud trees to surround this special area, selected to honor an aged redbud that was already starting to lose its will to live when we arrived. These, now mature and thriving, have proved to be worthy descendants of the original.

The original parcel had been subdivided before our clients bought their house, which now fronts the road created subsequently to connect additional house lots. The old carriage drive from the bridge led to a detached garage that bisected most of the plantable table land, which meant the ravine was the only real landscape feature on the property. By removing the garage, we gained space to create a large lawn and a terraced overlook where the parents could observe their children and dogs. The original coach house remained standing nearby, but with a parcel in between, which was used to build another house. A few years after our initial project was completed, the clients were able to buy the house between the two historic structures and asked us to create a backyard for the kids. We worked to incorporate this found space into the existing landscape, including productive elements: a grape arbor so Bill could always make his famous recipe for dolmas, a vegetable garden, and even a chicken coop—the perfect pairing for successful "harvestables." Various vegetables were attempted over the years, but with the omnipresent rodent population in the wooded ravine, we eventually decided to focus on herbs, dahlias, and zinnias in the fenced-in area.

Carolyn will always equate an abundance of flowers with happiness, so we developed cultivated areas to hold butterfly bush, Russian sage, German irises, hydrangeas, 'William Baffin' roses, and Kentucky wisteria. We enclosed the space to allow children and dogs can run freely and to protect the blooms and vegetables from deer. This unique property satisfies with its mix of cultivated and wild elements for any mood, at different topographic levels.

Verdant moss covers New York fieldstones among spring woodland flowers, including *Mertensia virginica*, *Epimedium sulphureum* and *E. rubrum*, to name a few.

Above: The original house and the fieldstone addition overlook the garden below and ravine beyond. *Opposite:* An ancient Redbud is preserved with the support of a forked branch.

Overleaf: Early summer at the top of the ravine with *Carex elata* 'Bowles Golden', *Corydalis lutea* and *C. ochroleuca* below and *Hydrangea petiolaris* growing on an old stump above.

Screen planting with *Physocarpus x* 'Monlo', Rosa 'William Baffin', and *Weigela x* 'Wine and Roses' and the *Wisteria macrostachya* 'Aunt Dee' covered arbor.

Pennsylvania fieldstone boulder seating and steps with spring *Aquilegia canadensis* and *Corydalis* seedings.

Reimagined Gardens

Nepeta 'Blue Wonder' emerges from a Victorian-era child's iron bench.

Requests for reinterpreting a green space can come from many different directions, but there are three main drivers: a garden owner decides to rework an existing garden, a garden we've been tending for years is sold to a new owner, or clients import us to help with a distant home they've just bought.

If a client requests dramatic changes or a whole new theme, we encourage them not to throw everything away and start over, and that extends to existing plants, hardscape materials, and garden ornaments. Even if there are drastically different new plans in mind, the odds are that some of the established plantings can be reused. There is value in context, history, and nuance; all are important to preserve.

We are able to set aside previous expectations and focus on reinterpreting the possibilities for making spaces work with a new plan. Our team will always have emotional attachments to a few favorite plants in every garden, but we can be stoic professionals and play nonpartisan politics to save only the most important players. New programs often involve a change to the color palette, the bloom schedule (to adapt to an owner's new travel schedules), or major structural adaptations to the plantings to address changes in the architecture.

We've found that, interestingly, it's often more difficult for us to adapt to the expectations of new clients who buy an existing garden than to rework an old project completely. Establishing a rapport is paramount to success. Walling off our old perspectives to embrace their new goals is a challenge when we've already poured time into making every inch of a green space sing, but we understand it's inevitable that a new owner will want to make changes to put their own stamp on the place. Experience and familiarity with a garden give us the ability to communicate what is possible in detail. For instance, if a property has deer pressure constraints but a client really hopes for tulips, we can suggest planting them where the deer are least likely to graze, such as in pots near the front porch. We have learned to be humble, to embrace garden refreshes as an opportunity to create new experiences—it can be exciting for all. Once we help clients understand that our first obligation is to the horticulture, not our original design, the process typically goes well.

Existing clients will often ask us to consult on a new house or a second home property too. That can be a less complex transition since we already understand each other, but developing a new garden style, driven by very different architecture, a vastly different climate, the amount of time they're planning to spend at the property, or a complete lifestyle change can mean just as much work as starting from scratch, which surprises some clients.

We are not so arrogant about what we have done with gardens that we can't adapt, or tailor things to suit new needs or ideas. We speak "plant" to help the client understand the possibilities on any given site and work toward a successful, collaborative solution between people and plants. Environmentally speaking, we are constantly working on reinterpreting past ideas too, so in some cases a request to revise a garden we designed a decade ago, or longer, can help make it more sustainable since our understanding of and adherence to sustainable practices continues to evolve.

New Life for an Old Stable

We have been working with this property, originally part of a grand estate in Lake Forest, since 2000, so it's become one of our nearest and dearest projects. The current house was a former stable, and originally had a greenhouse attached at the rear. A dilapidated shed stored a small English convertible. These structures were perched right at the edge of a natural ravine. The ravine runs along the entire northeast edge of the property, and a remnant orchard plot lies to the east, which acts as the main yard for this charming and historical house.

At about the same time we were asked to rethink the landscape, the clients commissioned architect Thomas J. Rajkovich to enlarge the garage and add an upstairs office. Charles Fischer and Craig were ecstatic to see he had already included a potting shed as part of the complex. The beautiful details, proportion, and scale of the structure are a tribute to Tom's great classical training. It all blended seamlessly with the original stable building, everything clad in reclaimed Chicago common brick. Unfortunately, just before the new building was completed, there was a violent August hailstorm that severely damaged the original slate roof on the stable and, ultimately, meant it needed to be replaced. For us this provided an opportunity to simultaneously re-roof both structures in new Vermont gray slate, for visual continuity. No one saw that coming!

The husband already had a substantial rose garden, begun with transplants from his mother's, so these plants were particularly prized by the family. To retain them and give them prominence, we planted them at the perimeter of the space. We conceived a central sunken garden that would act as a sort of formal frame and foreground them in the long view from the new terrace into the orchard beyond. This is the longest viewshed on the property, so we capitalized on it by siting a welcoming bench up the slight rise. To keep the roses alive during construction, we dug them up and moved them to our nursery facility for four months—not one perished! The sunken area also allowed us to improve the drainage around them by draining excess water directly into the ravine instead of letting it pool on flat ground. An adjacent new terrace occupies the footprint of the original greenhouse, long since demolished. We covered its slab and old foundation with bluestone and added a verdigris-colored Old Westbury Gardens–inspired wooden arbor for wisteria.

Eventually, the owners decided to downsize; just a few weeks later, another of our clients called me and asked what we thought of this exact property. Our reply? "It has a really beautiful garden!" A month later, they bought the place and began making it their own. The new owners fully embraced what had been done, but they were interested in embellishing what had been started. That meant a few more alterations from Tom Rajkovich and CBLD, and they also decided to hire Paul Klug for the interior renovations and outdoor furnishings. They requested a quiet dining space on the rooftop overlooking the ravine, so we added lightweight fiberglass containers along the rail and made a perimeter of low color. The addition of lounge and dining furniture ensures it gets heavy summertime use.

When the last of the old orchard trees died, we decided to change the way the main lawn space was used. It's now home to a progressively planted arboretum of specimen trees—the new owner's passion. The first big celebration held there was their eldest daughter's rehearsal dinner, and in subsequent years, many family events have been held under a tent nestled between its lush foliage and abundant flowers.

The original owners had asked for a small cutting garden behind the garage to supply fresh blooms for the house from May to November, so we populated it with lilacs, delphiniums, cosmos, dahlias, peonies, snapdragons, daisies, basil, and a rainbow of zinnias, to name a few. The new owners expanded this by a hundred and twenty feet, and it can now be seen from all east facing windows. The planting also include peonies and phlox, moved over from the garden we designed at their former house. The couple had never tried flower arranging or gardening before, and they've learned to love it in retirement, proving that we, like gardens, can continue to evolve beautifully.

Reclaimed brick piers piers with stone birds of prey signal the entrance to the stone path along the top of the ravine.

Previous spread: Garden maidens immersed in profuse, high-summer bloom.
Opposite, top: A massive Moroccan vessel filled with *Plumbago auriculata* 'Escapade Blue' is a transition between the cutting garden and the lawn.

Opposite, bottom: The strong linear lines of layered hedges work as backdrop for the Sunken Garden and screen a maintenance path.
Above: A verdigris Wisteria trellis frames ravine views in contrast to the formal "reverse" box and bluestone parterre in foreground.

A Reverence for Site

Our team had driven by this lovely, well-appointed house many times over the years, and we had always been curious about what its gardens might look like. We had only managed tantalizing glimpses of old balustrades, gravel paths, and a sunken garden from a charity house-walk event, so when the owner called to invite us to collaborate on refreshing the gardens, we accepted immediately.

The house was designed by Howard Van Doren Shaw in 1912, with his now-classic elements such as a welcoming twelve-foot-wide drive, entry columns, and hand-wrought fencing. The building sits on just over two acres—and a full quarter acre is devoted to the splendid formal sunken garden. Its rose garden and man-made water lily ponds were long renowned in the area, and a few still exist today. This client was more interested in setting a color scheme for the flowers and helping everything meld together than in dictating how to use planting bed space, giving Donald Bolak and Craig a free hand to invent revised, up-to-date uses for the upper and lower spaces.

A charming reoccurring motif, seen in the masonry in various locations, is a mixed bouquet, or "compote," of flowers—a perfect element for us to carry into the garden as ornament as well. The main terrace, its historical central water tank for water lilies, and its carved-stone fountain feature are visible from the bay window in the formal dining room, so we attended to minor restoration work needed there immediately. A screened porch that dominates the west end of the terrace made us very nostalgic for earlier times when people seemingly had many more free hours to just sit and relax (even if they didn't have the benefit of air-conditioning). The east end of the terrace features a glazed garden room that overlooks the sunken garden.

The cohesion between the house and this garden makes its already elegant architecture feel even more beautiful, thanks to original design details that we worked to preserve and hopefully enhance. A brick stair leads to the two-tier terraced area and grotto fountain in a way that can only be described as genteel; we added appropriately scaled accent shrubbery to either side and a creeping tapestry of plants in the center. The balustrade surrounding the garden practically called out for vining clematis of all forms and bloom times. The formal space all but whispered to us that it could use a boxwood parterre; we added one and helped it embrace a pair of old yew mounds that had survived decades. Even in the winter, this garden is beautiful thanks to the structure of the evergreens and the masonry architectural ornaments. We reactivated the pergola with containers, antique lanterns, and furniture to lure people down from the house and encourage them to linger in the garden. The soft colors of the perennial garden's flowers continue through the seasons, accented by spring and summer's tulips, *Salvia, Digitalis,* and *Dahlia*. Nora Kennedy's artistic eye has been an integral part of the continued success of this garden, as well as contributions by many others at the firm.

What we celebrate the most about this space is the grade change integral to this original garden. It is so much more dynamic and interesting than if it were flat, and yet in today's gardens, these have fallen out of fashion. In the Midwest we have few hills, so slopes excite us. This site is on a piece of table land that ultimately drains to a nearby ravine, and we're in awe that Shaw saw the opportunity to capitalize on the terrain. It's so difficult to engineer great architectural moves that link a structure with the land so well.

Delphinium 'Blue Jay' and *Rosa* 'Ballerina' at the steps to the Sunken Garden.

The addition of the surrounding path anchors the original balustrade and is softened by Clematis and tumblers. The six existing wall buttresses at the far end were enhanced by a set of cast-stone compotes.

Top left: View across the Walled Garden to the figure of Hebe from the upper landing of the steps to the house. *Bottom left:* View from the main terrace to the restored trellis enclosures in the Sunken Garden.

Right: From this vantage point the Sunken Garden leads up to the thyme panel landing, then the turf terrace up to the garden room lookout. *Overleaf:* Reimagined pergola and fence.

A Gardener's Garden

It's a challenge, sometimes, as a garden designer, not to pull over during a drive to try and peer over hedges or walls at some of the North Shore's estates, but that sort of thing can be frowned upon. This property, in particular, tormented us for years, keeping its secrets. In this case, though, we now know we could have just knocked on the door and been welcomed in—owner Loreen Mershimer's passion for gardens is equal to or greater than anyone's at CBLD. Her fall season ends on her knees planting hundreds, if not thousands, of spring-flowering bulbs. She starts seeds compulsively in February, under grow lights in the basement. She places her massive seasonal plant orders at various custom growers, and then in late April starts her hunt-and-gather visits to local nurseries, greenhouses, and big-box stores. Loreen does not discriminate about where a plant is purchased, only if it is healthy and a good fit for her garden.

The Garden Conservancy Open Days program has helped enthusiasts visit beautiful private gardens across the country, and many of our clients' gardens have been included. Loreen had herself visited the great Camp Rosemary in Lake Forest several years in succession during those open days and aspired to interpret its wonders for herself in some way. She called Craig and Erin Marie Herrera soon after purchasing this property; she came in with a historic site plan, images, and lists to help guide us through her dream garden themes. Loreen could recognize openly what she didn't know about design, however, and was quite content to focus her own efforts on seasonal displays and the ongoing care for the garden—she left it to us to expand and enhance garden areas across the property.

Together we conceived a planting bed configuration throughout the property as Loreen's dream garden. These spaces are visible from the house year-round. The upper rear yard is shared with her neighbor to the west, so cooperative planting flanks a now-inactive water feature ruin that benefits both; it can be seen from their respective terraces.

The main garden is in fact Loreen's half of a shared sunken garden; in 1923, architect Philip Brooks Maher built adjoining houses for his two daughters, as wedding presents. In Loreen's space, a center island bed edged in step-over espaliers features an extensive collection of hardy perennials and roses. Years before, we had planted a central bed of pink shrub roses edged in boxwood for a simple, elegant statement on the adjoining property; now it seemed like serendipity that the spaces could talk to each other. Loreen's previously groundcover-planted slopes are filled with short-statured flowering shrub masses and easier-care perennial plants. From either terrace, the views of the sunken garden with the gardens on the upper level are nothing but spectacular from spring through late summer. A treat to visit, this garden is now shared with garden groups of all kinds, notably during the period-appropriate *Great Gatsby* garden fête celebrating the house's one hundredth birthday.

Remnant water-feature rockery now separates the two properties.

Above: This bird's-eye view reveals the relationship of the house to the street, the entry pavilion to the sunken space, and the matrix of paths connecting the house to the garden.

Opposite, top: The entry pavilion overlooks the sunken space. *Opposite, bottom:* The original slopes were altered to colorful perennial plantings that frame the stairs to the upper gardens beyond.

Overleaf: A moment when we can see perfection within reach.

A Botanist's Garden

We met these clients just a few years before Little Orchard, their beautiful house designed by Howard Van Doren Shaw, celebrated its hundredth birthday. We had just enough time to revive the existing walled garden, originally designed by Ellen Biddle Shipman in the early 1910s, before the party to celebrate that milestone. The owner was a trained botanist from Philadelphia's Main Line. She missed the gentler climate of the East Coast, but she had found that the historical brick wall insulated the garden from the brutal shore winds of Lake Michigan and captured the lake's beneficial temperature mediation, creating a microclimate almost identical to that of her former home.

Craig and Charles Fischer were fortunate to be able to work with incredible historical plants including a two-hundred-year-old native red oak, a hundred-year-old climbing hydrangea, and an incredible espaliered saucer magnolia—something we had never seen! We took care not to do too much planting under the canopy or root zone of the heritage red oak. A grove of *Betula* 'White Spire' birch provides balance along with a mature Norway spruce to the south, and all sheltered the thirty-foot-long old climbing hydrangea as well as a new collection of rhododendrons and mountain laurel. A hellebore collection along the log-round steppingstone path adds mid-range height to the naturally mossy, verdant space.

We broke through the upper terrace wall—an inadvisable addition of some years earlier, and installed broad bluestone steps to create display space for containers where the client can grow specimens of unique plants, hardy and not. These plants, real horticultural goodies, are entries in local garden club competitions focused on personal plant collections in containers. The northern of the two large planting beds visible from the patio features a palette of blue, yellow, and white. This is represented in flora and foliage from glaucus silvers to the most vivid chartreuses, and delphiniums take center stage in June. The southern bed, in contrast, is an abundance of burgundies, strong pinks, and reds. All these tones, with a backdrop of lustrous green foliage, create stunning moments.

Over several years, we intentionally used the same species of plants in seasonally planted containers, then added them to drifts of the same plant back in the beds once their season of interest had faded. *Dicentra spectabilis* 'Alba' and *Adiantum pedatum*, for example, were combined in spring containers and then relocated under the bench in the arbor. A favorite summer memory was seeing the maidenhair fern fronds happily growing up through the seat of the bench—we all appreciated that fern's fortitude. Plants will always tell us where they are happiest. The *Persicaria affinis* 'Darjeeling Red' that was planted on the edge of the red bed worked its way over the edging and into the gravel path, where it performed phenomenally. So we left it. Who are we to decide?

The reconfigured garden has four large planting beds, each with a bisecting path for strolling and care access. The central feature is a box and barberry parterre. (The barberry is a sterile cultivar.) Brick-a-brack bed edging was requested by the client. The owner, a mad collector of woody plants, also charged us with highlighting woody treasures, pushing the climate zone, and complementing all of it with herbaceous perennial materials.

Adapting hardscape elements to the historical setting meant taking care to reuse what was in situ, or to match original details. A rectangular water tank on axis with the view to the lake was refurbished to hold waterlilies and papyrus, for example. Ill-fitting modern steps and hardscape additions over the years were removed if deemed a mismatch with the overall aesthetic. The owner's mantra guided us: "When it falls down, then we will fix it right for the next hundred years." The grades around the north garden gate had been altered by driveway renovations, so this opportunity allowed us to introduce an arced step and landing, designed to look as if it was the original entry to this secret garden space.

In working on old homes and gardens, we have learned that repairs and restorations are only as good as the craftsperson or artisan who does the work; Fernando Guidarini and his skilled team performed all the vital masonry on this project, and it still looks wonderful decades later. Charles Fischer also worked with Craig on the sensitive reinterpretation of the space and its plant collection, but this garden has been one of Russ's true fascinations. He enjoyed an informed client, the site, and the fact that the garden wasn't all herbaceous perennials. We were always trying new things to see if they would survive, thanks to the wall, so it served as a virtual greenhouse for us too, in a way. This garden's future is now under a new family's care. They truly own a treasure of a house and garden.

Picea pungens glauca 'Globosa', Weigela x florida 'Variegata' and Lysimachia nummularia 'Aurea' create a blue, yellow, and white palette.

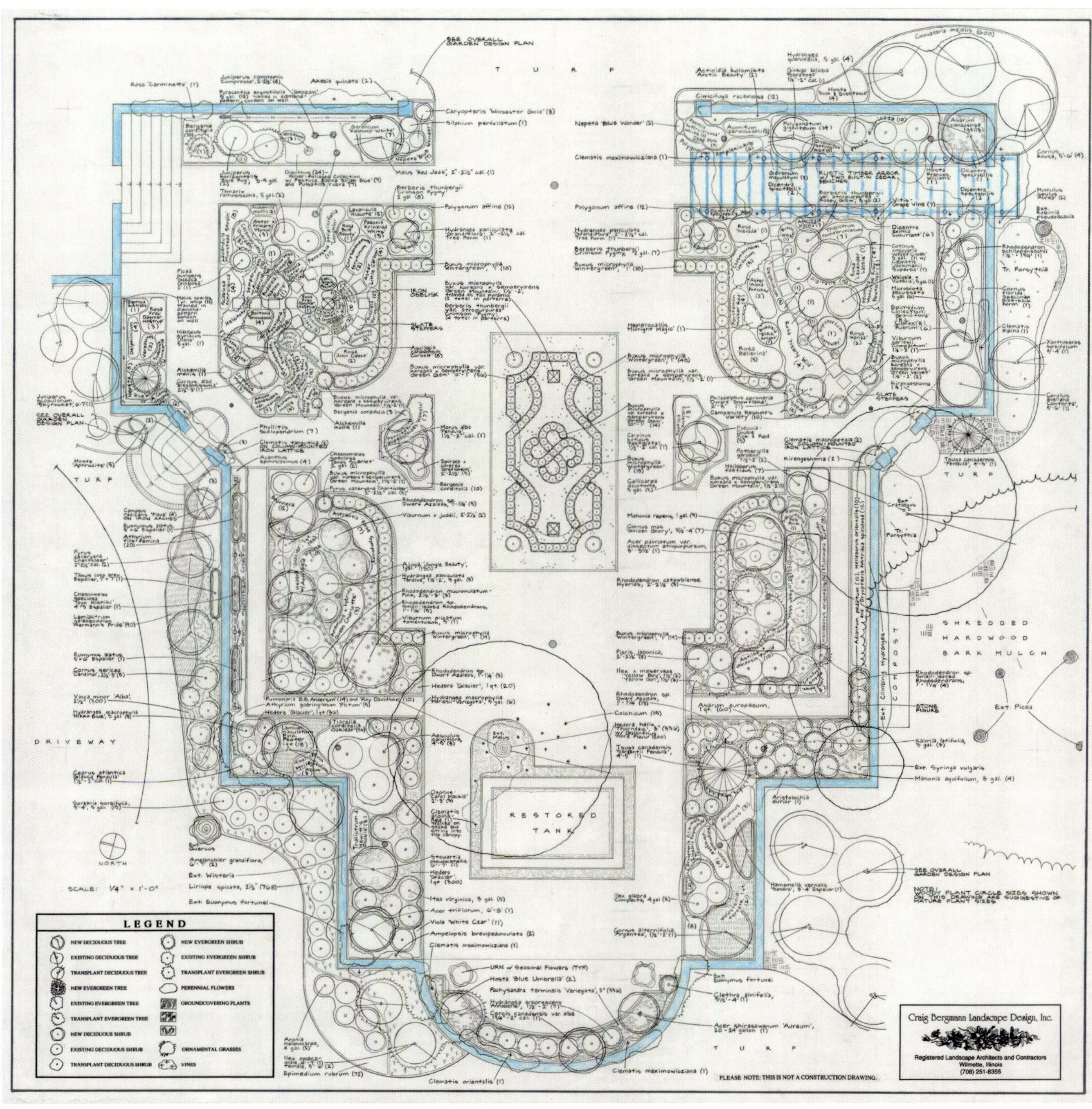

Opposite, top: View across the Walled Garden to the entry gate.
Opposite, bottom: An ancient climbing hydrangea drapes over the opposite gate with weeping *Tsuga canadensis sargentii*, *Kirengishoma palmata*, and *Primula japonica* in a pink, purple, and burgundy palette.

Above: Walled Garden planting plan.

Perspective across the boxwood parterre to the glorious *Viburnum plicatum var. tomentosum* 'Mariesii'.

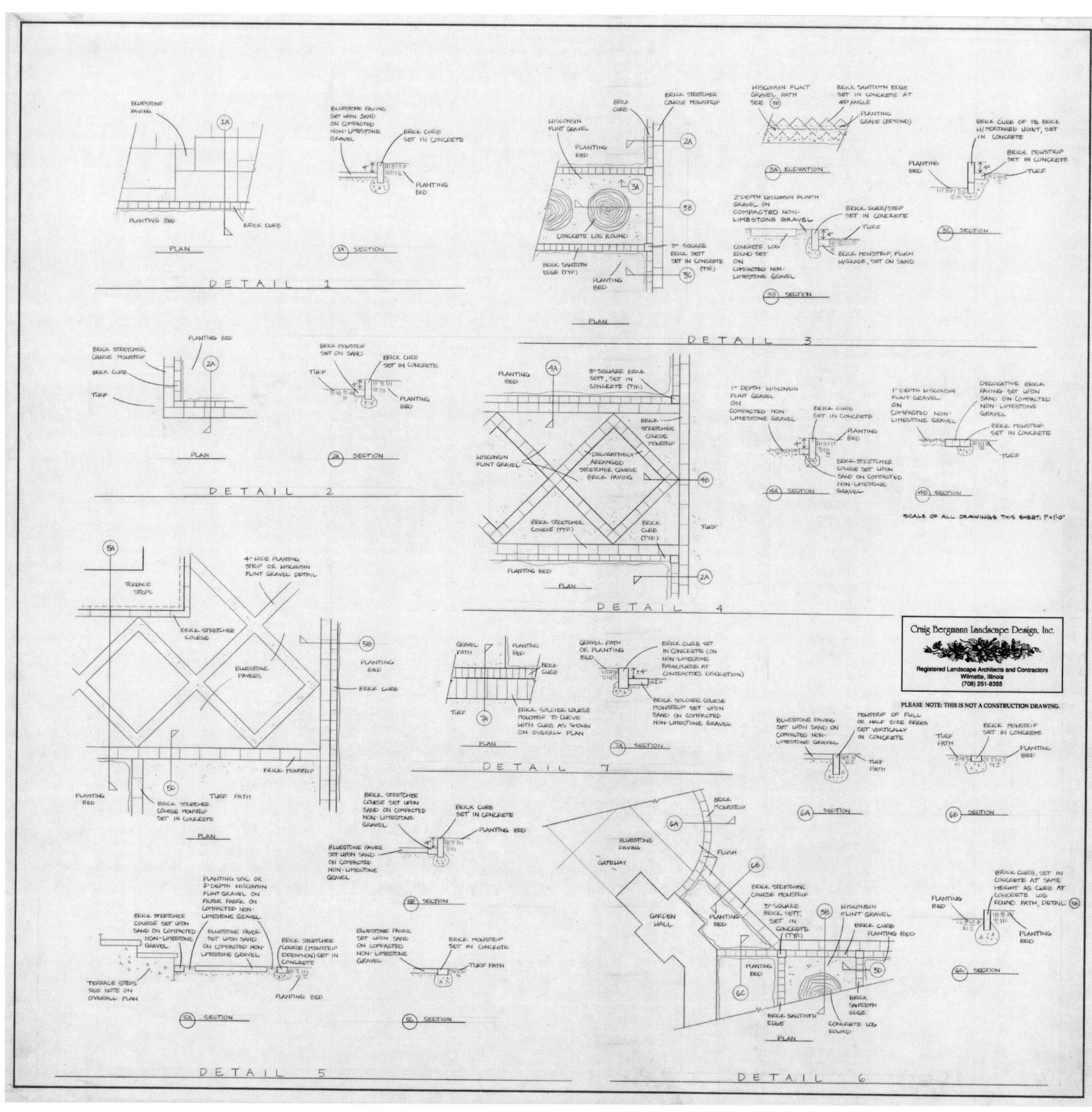

Above: Masonry details for paths and edges.

Opposite, top: Old crabapple tree over the waterlily tank with clambering *Clematis paniculata* in summer. ***Opposite, bottom:*** View over the tank to the seating area at lilac-flowering time.

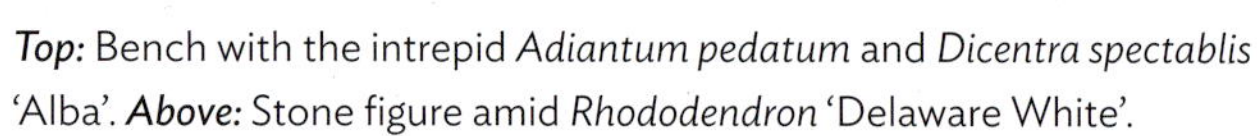

Top: Bench with the intrepid *Adiantum pedatum* and *Dicentra spectablis* 'Alba'. ***Above:*** Stone figure amid *Rhododendron* 'Delaware White'.

Above: Rustic raw-cedar grape arbor over a gravel and brick path.

Manse Garden

Everyone who travels through the North Shore towns notices this elegant property sooner or later. Giant stone gateposts and a pair of mansard-roofed coach houses frame a view down the drive to this elegant, stately home set atop the bluff overlooking Lake Michigan. The owners visited our gardens in Lake Forest at Paul's invitation since they had all been friends for years and he knew the husband had always loved beautiful gardens. He thought that showing them our Gardens at 900 might inspire him with some new possibilities for their property. Erin Marie Herrera and Craig went on to develop a plan to revamp their existing walled garden, various details throughout the larger garden, and the swimming pool area.

The property already held numerous planted containers; we reorganized some to accentuate sitting areas and direct views. Because this is such a large property with already intensive maintenance needs, we contained our beautification projects in specific, controlled areas so as not to add much more to the tending requirements.

The walled garden is situated on the opposite side of the house from the lake, creating a protected area from its sometimes-brutal winds. Our vision was to capitalize on the views from various of the French doors into the space by adding beds at the corners of the central lawn area that would include more flowers for more color. We also installed a central fountain to to add subtle sparkle and movement to the space.

At the other extreme, the unsheltered swimming pool terrace received sunlight so intense it made it inhospitable. Care of the gardens here required Linda Miranda and her team to plan their schedule around the most intense conditions during the day. We constructed a pergola with columns of stacked Ludovici terra-cotta roof tiles—leftover from hailstorm repairs on the main house roof. We topped these with limestone cornices, then added a canopy of oak timbers and wrought iron. To save the ancient wisteria vine that was growing on the original back wall, we constructed a temporary scaffolding to support it and then carefully blanketed the new pergola with its branches once all work had been completed. A satisfying moment to see the new structure look as if it had supported the vine for years! Those kinds of details make all the difference when working toward making a new project fit into historic context.

The form of the early twentieth-century pool pavilion is softened by espalier trained over the years to encircle the window.

Previous spread: The bluff edge, source of the name of the house, is planted with *Echinacea purpurea* and *Schizachyrium scoparium*.
Below, left: The entrance to the manor house is flanked by pillars of Pelargoniums and Verbenas.

Below, top right: A luxuriant border of Dahlias, Buddleias, *Hibiscus syriacus* 'Blue Satin' and *Hydrangea paniculata* 'Limelight' standards in August.
Below, bottom right: The central fountain in the West Garden; the sunroom parterre is beyond.

Previous spread: Summer spectacle in the West Garden with glazed terra-cotta figures of the Four Seasons. ***Above:*** Conceptual renderings of West Garden (top) and the Pool Garden.

Opposite, top: Pool Garden border plants were selected for long summer bloom, persistent foliage, and short stature to allow for clear views across the pool. ***Opposite, bottom:*** Newly conceived pergola with Ludowici terra-cotta roofing tile columns and an oak-and-iron canopy supports ancient Wisteria preserved from an earlier structure.

Layering

Over the years, we have developed favorite plant combinations. We focus on ways to combine different plants, pair a selected object with a plant, or on a grand scale, pair trees with a structure. This is all part of our day-to-day work, generally with the aim of extending seasonal interest. The occasional punctuation of a plant or two in the middle of a mass or matrix planting scheme throws the two into such heightened contrast that it creates something much more texturally interesting than either could ever be alone. This type of detail is our sweet spot when it comes to ruminating in the gardens we tend. A garden is never truly finished, so we are constantly scrutinizing what we see in attempt to bring the level up another notch on the beauty scale.

Layering is one of our favorite ways to get multiple combinations out of one space. We strive to have multiple seasons of interest from our gardens. For example, we plan for bulbs to pop up just as perennials are emerging. It is not enough to interplant bulbs such as *Narcissus* or *Allium* with daylily or an ornamental grass for extended color alone, however. Spring-flowering bulb plants play off the subtle coloration of emergent perennial foliage; as they senesce and fade, the fully flushed perennial foliage conceals their retreat. Peonies are notable for their beautiful burgundy early spring stems, which then turn to a stalwart dark green foliage—a great companion plant for an added ephemeral splash of white and blue. By planting *Galanthus* and *Leucojum* with *Muscari*, or *Scilla hispanica* at the base of the plant, we get a long and interesting combination. Adding *Lilium* and *Lycoris* in between the plants extends the color effect, even in a small space, for months. Even the typical negative space of turf can come alive in spring if it's planted with crocus or other minor bulbs such as *Tulipa* sylvatica or even *Narcissus*. In late summer, planting *Cochicum* or saffron crocus can also be effective, if the lawn is not too irrigated.

Moments like this allow for flowering focal points to change throughout the year, keeping the garden interesting as we go out to look and see what's new each day.

A palette of blue, yellow, and white with dahlias, panicle hydrangea, and the late sky-blue of *Salvia azurea*.

Informal Gardens

Opposite: *Clematis x jackmanii* 'Superba' rambling through rustic pickets.

When we think about gardens whose overall mood is meant to help you feel relaxed, the design is often less formal, taking inspiration from the natural world instead of the built environment of the site. The plan still includes elements that are carefully organized to link to the cultivated world, and the connection to the house is paramount. This space is designed to blend the architecture with the garden as if the built structures grew and developed along with the plants. The design is intended to direct attention to the unexpected; the focus might be an ancient oak, a beautiful ravine, or a vista.

Hardscape elements are often more organic in form or at least in shape. Less rigid paving lines softened by tumblers on the edges helps to paint the informality of the space. During bed layout we usually consider the use of curvilinear bed lines to evoke this informality, and we often expand the sense of space by keeping the eye from seeing all the edges at once. The plant palette is often simpler to emphasize on the open spaces for calm and there are few if any, heavily pruned elements. The plant collection should never seem disorganized or confusing; it should be flowing with smooth transitions through repetition.

Special collections of plants and moments are strategically placed. The overall experience is balanced with the linking effect of negative space of turf or meadow plantings. Blurring a property line with loose plantings also provides the feeling of expansiveness.

Family Compound

This project expanded a property in an already well-developed neighborhood to create an insulated family compound. When Erin Marie Herrera and Craig met the clients, they had just become owners of the main house; a neighboring property came on the market soon afterward—in an unfortunate state—but it was an opportune moment for them to buy it. The house on the adjacent property was demolished, and Northworks Architecture was retained to create a guesthouse that could also serve as a place for entertaining. Requests for casual use included a screened porch, a covered porch for watching kids at play, and adjoining patios. The main property already had a pool, so the expansion was intended to provide lots of space for child's play, a winter ice rink, and a fire pit for gatherings. The pandemic hit, and the new guesthouse quickly became a schoolhouse for our clients' children and a few neighborhood friends who lived nearby.

A few years later, the owners were able to purchase a third adjacent property; it held a wonderful old house and a native woodland. This allowed the family to move the husband's parents to the compound. They absolutely loved to garden—a bonus. As the children have grown, much of the original lawn space has been converted to large islands of shrubs and perennial plantings. This repurposing reduces stress on the older trees and native fauna that were trying to grow in the presence of a chemically treated lawn. We linked the three properties via woodland transitions, which has helped in reestablishing the natural understory plantings and nestled the compound into the landscape.

We created a fenced vegetable garden to the northwest of the guesthouse, contained in a collection of galvanized horse troughs to provide raised beds for ease of tending—and to keep us from having to dig in the subterranean drainage vault system we had to create for compensatory storm water storage, a requirement of the local municipality as part of property redevelopment permitting. The productive area is a wonderful shared space for the multi-generational family.

The clients are deeply involved in the management of the property, with unwavering focus to see that the space is preserved properly with correct watering, professional arborist care to help maintain a large white oak grove, and collaborating with us to let the plantings mature appropriately without over-pruning. The beauty-making was our job, and we feel we have built a gracious homestead for a wonderful family.

A serpentine stone wall defines the subtle grade change.

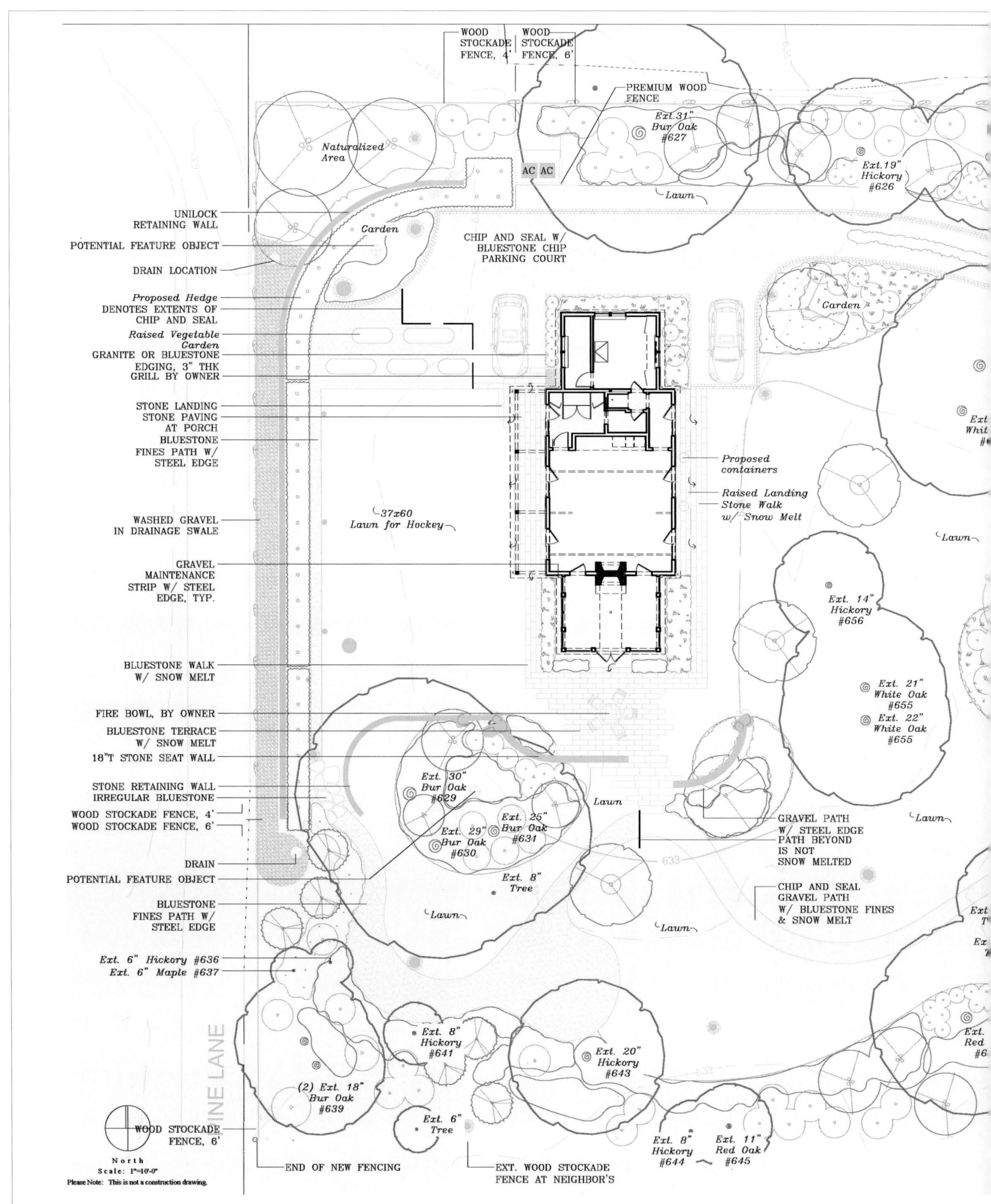

WOOD STOCKADE FENCE, 4'
WOOD STOCKADE FENCE, 6'
PREMIUM WOOD FENCE
Ext.31" Bur Oak #627
Naturalized Area
AC AC
Ext.19" Hickory #626
Lawn
UNILOCK RETAINING WALL
Garden
POTENTIAL FEATURE OBJECT
CHIP AND SEAL W/ BLUESTONE CHIP PARKING COURT
DRAIN LOCATION
Proposed Hedge
DENOTES EXTENTS OF CHIP AND SEAL
Garden
Raised Vegetable Garden
GRANITE OR BLUESTONE EDGING, 3" THK
GRILL BY OWNER
STONE LANDING
STONE PAVING AT PORCH
BLUESTONE FINES PATH W/ STEEL EDGE
Proposed containers
Raised Landing Stone Walk w/ Snow Melt
WASHED GRAVEL IN DRAINAGE SWALE
37x60 Lawn for Hockey
Lawn
GRAVEL MAINTENANCE STRIP W/ STEEL EDGE, TYP.
Ext. 14" Hickory #656
BLUESTONE WALK W/ SNOW MELT
Ext. 21" White Oak #655
Ext. 22" White Oak #655
FIRE BOWL, BY OWNER
BLUESTONE TERRACE W/ SNOW MELT
18"T STONE SEAT WALL
STONE RETAINING WALL
IRREGULAR BLUESTONE
Ext. 30" Bur Oak #629
Lawn
WOOD STOCKADE FENCE, 4'
WOOD STOCKADE FENCE, 6'
Ext. 29" Bur Oak #630
Ext. 25" Bur Oak #631
GRAVEL PATH W/ STEEL EDGE PATH BEYOND IS NOT SNOW MELTED
Lawn
DRAIN
POTENTIAL FEATURE OBJECT
Ext. 8" Tree
633
CHIP AND SEAL GRAVEL PATH W/ BLUESTONE FINES & SNOW MELT
BLUESTONE FINES PATH W/ STEEL EDGE
Lawn
Lawn
Ext. 6" Hickory #636
Ext. 6" Maple #637
Ext. 8" Hickory #641
Ext. 20" Hickory #643
(2) Ext. 18" Bur Oak #639
Ext. 6" Tree
INE LANE
WOOD STOCKADE FENCE, 6'
Ext. 8" Hickory #644
Ext. 11" Red Oak #645
North
Scale: 1"=10'-0"
Please Note: This is not a construction drawing.
END OF NEW FENCING
EXT. WOOD STOCKADE FENCE AT NEIGHBOR'S

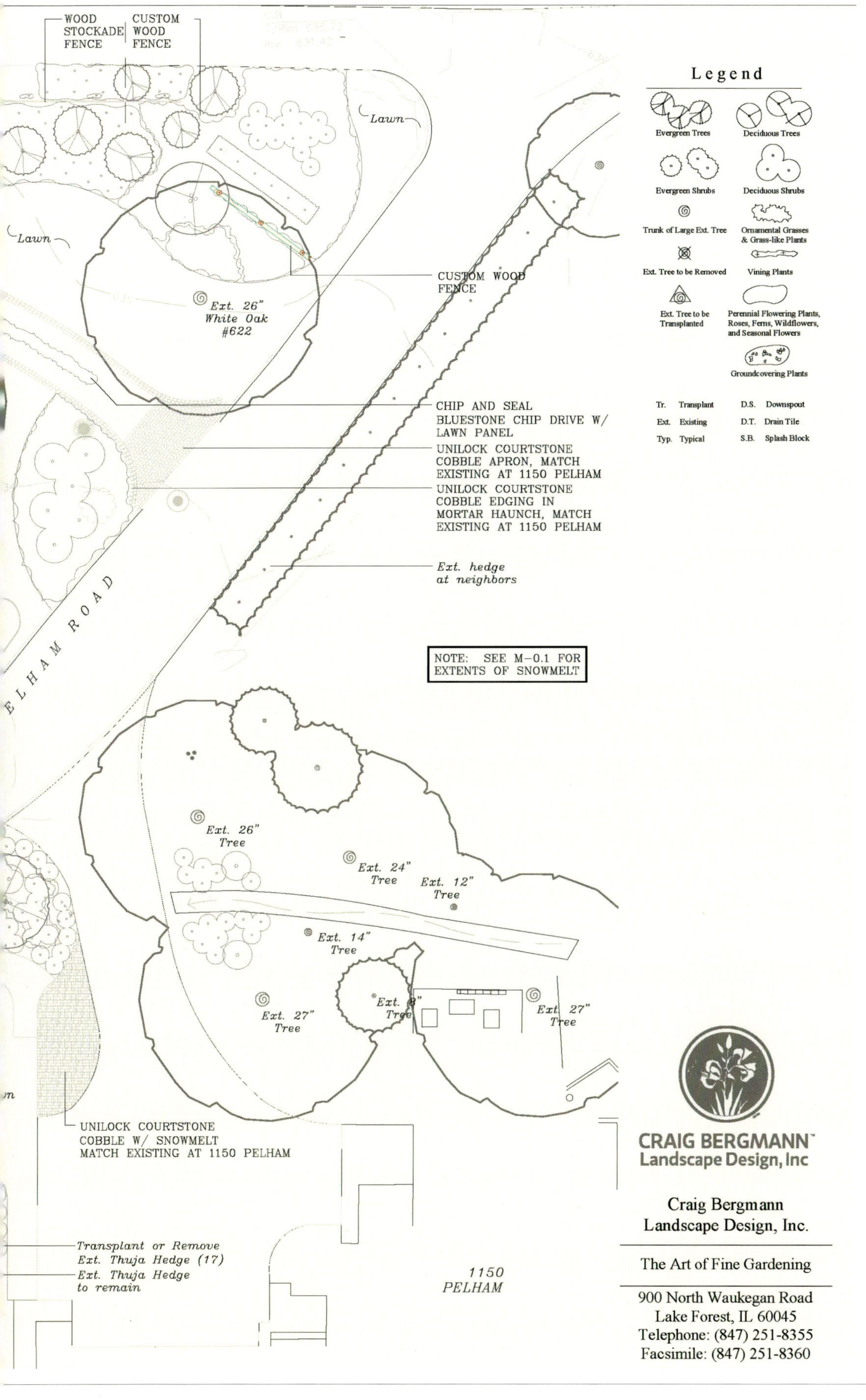

Comprehensive landscape plan.

Above: A gravel path leads from main drive to guest house. This path is heated during the winter. *Opposite, top:* A carved-stone watering trough reimagined as planter welcomes each season with new planting, backed by a steel and reclaimed-barn-timber wall.

Opposite, bottom: Three paving materials: formal bluestone, Belgian block, and crushed bluestone chip. All sympathetic in color tone, each provides the appropriate support for various activities. *Overleaf:* Limestone spheres punctuate the sinuous path to the main house.

A Collector's Paradise

We've been fortunate to work on this property for more than two decades, with two different owners—a pleasure and a privilege. It is a testament to both of the owners' fortitude and passion to commit to preserving such an incredible house and site. The woman who built the house in 1929 had an extensive art collection, with a focus on American folk art. She was friends with Abby Aldrich Rockefeller, who founded the American Folk Art Museum in New York City, and she and her husband contributed the best of their collection to the then-new museum. Such an owner would hardly be content with an average house. Our current clients are also avid collectors of folk art, garden objects, vintage globes, curiosities, and antique Indian silks.

Originally, the house was clad in a bright-white stucco with dark-brown windows and decorative plaster detailing. A black asphalt roof topped off its gables and wings, making it look like something out of a European village. Charles Fischer and Craig had just started designing the perennial planting plan for the main garden when the client returned from a family biking tour in the South of France; that trip inspired her to change the exterior color to umber and to install a rough cedar shake roof for a more textural, organic look. That, in turn, affected our planting plan. She also requested a pool, which required careful planning so it would not interfere with the main views from the house out to the pond. We found an underused part of the lawn that was on axis with the easternmost, single-story wing of the home where the pool could be placed; close enough for easy access but out of sight lines. A colony of old Pfitzer junipers had to be removed to allow for pool terracing. A new sneak-through staircase was built from the upper garden level to the pool. To screen the view of the pool from the entry, we added a new stucco wall coped with bluestone to mimic existing walls. This helped to conceal a new addition as well and visually link disparate parts of the house and gardens.

We erected a tall cedar pergola on the main lawn to shade a new bluestone patio and to support a now-gargantuan trumpet vine and sweet autumn clematis bramble. The main garden sits across from this patio, along the top and bottom of a low retaining wall that provides for great drainage, sun, and viewing of a medley of spring-through-fall, predominantly herbaceous plantings in myriad colors. This collection is designed to create an energetic juxtaposition against the calm of the pond beyond.

After the sale of the house to its present owners, we were asked to improve what was there and to continue bringing the property to its most relaxing state. The new owners like the south view from the dining room so much that they increased the height of its window, the better to see the main garden and patio from within the house. They asked us to expand the garden by the pool to provide a fenced-in cutting garden for their favorite flowers. A terra-cotta relief from Portland, Maine, was incorporated into the existing east pool wall for an artisanal touch.

We also upgraded the driveway with antique paver detailing and installed Wisconsin red flint in the entry circle surface. We walled the trash area behind a gated entry and added antique iron detailing to the basement stairwell—it's visible from the front entry approach to help provide period-appropriate style.

The west garden expanded as a celebration of shade plants. There, new weathered-stone columns fitted with an antique iron gate help to deter deer traffic. The clients also converted the screened porch to a year-round room so they could enjoy the old craggy apple trees that surround the porch, which we planted for the previous owners a decade before.

This ongoing love for a garden and commitment to collaboration is so rewarding. Roberto Hernandez has been the senior gardener on this project since our first interventions, and he, along with his crew, has become an immeasurable part of its enduring success. This reminds us all that the whole is greater than the sum of its parts.

Campsis x radicans blossoms scattered on a wet stone terrace.

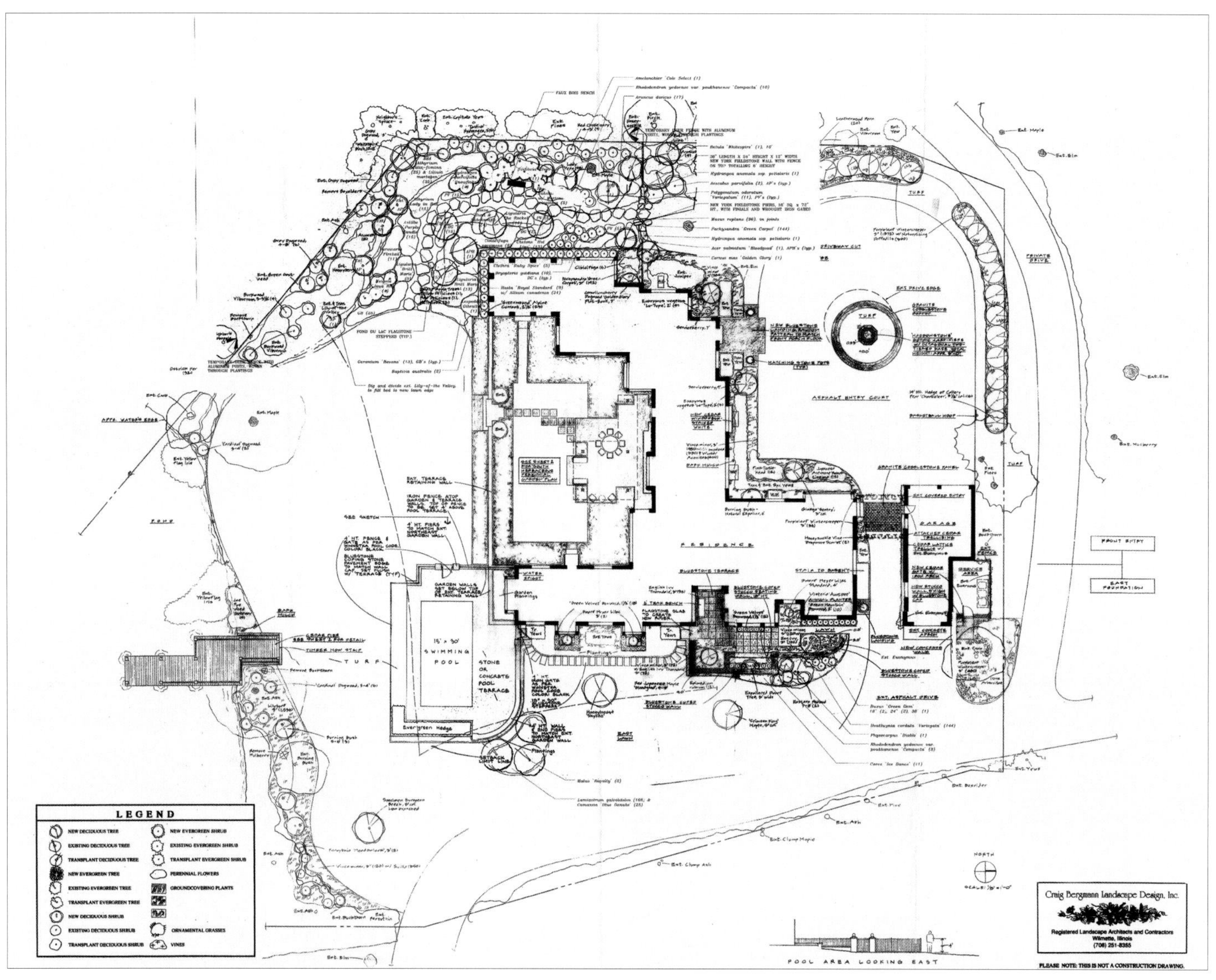

Above: Landscape plan. ***Opposite:*** False Spirea foliage contrasts with the pebble finish on the bench in this secluded place.

Overleaf: The Shade Garden in spring with emergent foliage of *Sorbaria sorbifolia* and *Acer palmatum* under flowering old apple trees.

Opposite, top: The entry is ornamented with an assemblage of stone peacocks, bench, and planted containers, celebrating the owners' love for collected art. *Opposite, bottom:* The structure of dormant *Campsis* provides an ethereal contrast to the emergent Crabapple trees beyond.

Above: View from the pool terrace to the upper garden space with a vine-covered pergola. *Overleaf:* A pastoral view across the adjoining spring-fed pond. All plantings are lightly placed to blur the line between cultivation and wild.

Left: *Astilbe taquetii* 'Superba' flanks the entrance to the Shade Garden from the lawn. ***Right:*** The secluded upper terrace is defined by the house and large yew balls, but paths lead out to various garden destinations, with floral abundance along the way.

Forty Years in a Garden

This project, Craig's first full-property commission, was the direct result of a response to a seasonal mailing we sent to a local grade school parents' list. Our sophisticated marketing tactic was to use a rubber stamp of a tree. It changed ink color for each season, accompanied a helpful garden-planning message: Apple green: "Time to plan and plant your seasonal flowers." Magenta: "Time to plan and plant your vegetable garden." Orange: "Time to plan and plant your spring-flowering bulbs." Purple: "Time to plan and plant your perennial garden." The owners of this house actually called us up! They asked if we could make their previously installed landscape slightly more casual, feeling a more relaxed landscape would be a better fit for their lifestyle. Craig made a hand-colored drawing to show them his ideas, and it worked. They set out to improve every inch of the property together.

An unassuming private road leads to the drive entrance here. The gardens are meant to be transitional passages through various outdoor living spaces; for example, a garden hidden behind the drive entry acts as focal point for the view from the house's sunroom. Upon leaving that outdoor space, the visitor will follow an intimate steppingstone path through a collection of shade-loving perennials whose abundantly interesting details, we hope, will cause them to move slowly through the space. This, in turn, opens onto an area designed to be appreciated best from the kitchen nook. Beyond is the outdoor terrace, capped by an arbor that overlooks a swimming pool and a colorful garden beyond. This bright outdoor space has a backdrop of mixed upright evergreens and native woodland plants as a calming foil.

As decades have passed, we've refined, changed, and added hardscape details. Most recently, we decided to remove the swimming pool, as it was receiving less and less use since the children were grown and flown, in favor of expanding the garden and taking advantage of what was its sunniest spot. A big hole in the clay subsoil remained after the pool was removed, so we had to re-create the right soil profile and drainage for the area from scratch; much like building a gravel-and-soil Napolean pastry or a hearty lasagna.

The clients' flower color palette has never varied, however. They continue to adore pale pinks and lavenders, blues, white, purples. Oranges and reds have never made an appearance here, except as plump berries or in fall foliage. Having spent four decades on this site, with the same owners, has yielded such exquisite pleasures in watching the property mature. Along the way, we have had to react to adjoining property construction to preserve the privacy of this site, and this has taught us that change is always healthy, whether it's initiated from desire, necessity, or practicality.

This garden also brings up one of our most poignant anecdotes. Craig had cajoled his way into buying one of the most spectacular *Rhododendron schlippenbachii* ever seen from a local nursery, when it had been destined for the White House! He begged the owners of Fiore Nursery to let him have it, and for whatever reason, they did. We planted it here, and it stayed beautiful for years—then the cicadas hatched as part of their seventeen-year life cycle. Little did we know this area was ground zero for the population boom. When Brood XIII, the largest of all, hatched, we learned the hard way that they do not mix with azaleas. In late May and early June, the insects emerged. In the month that they live, the females lay their eggs by cutting into the stems of plants. The damage to this plant appeared the next spring—the wounds dried out the stems, and by spring of the next season, the previous few years' growth was mostly dead. The plant bravely sent out advantageous buds below the wounds, but it never recovered. All to say that in considering what to plant, take cicadas into account if you live in a cicada breeding area! There is a happy ending: we were able to turn this setback into an opportunity for change. The area now houses a beautiful Hydrangea mass.

Gravel terrace with a pergola at the garden edge.

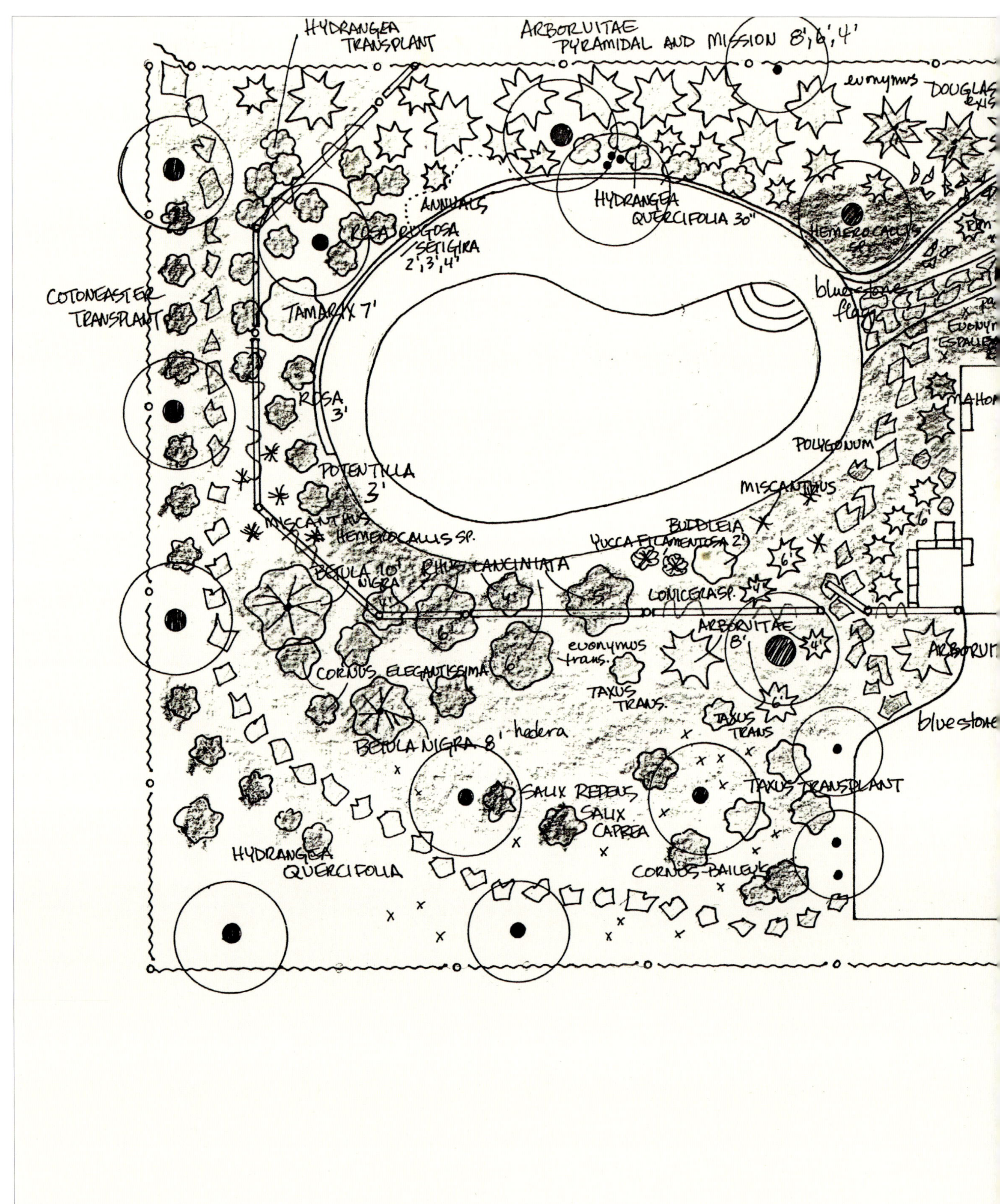
HYDRANGEA
TRANSPLANT
ARBORVITAE
PYRAMIDAL AND MISSION 8', 6', 4'
euonymus
DOUGLAS
ANNUALS
HYDRANGEA
QUERCIFOLIA 30"
HEMEROCALLIS SP.
ROSA RUGOSA
SETIGIRA
2', 3', 4'
COTONEASTER
TRANSPLANT
TAMARIX 7'
bluestone
flags
ROSA
3'
POLYGONUM
POTENTILLA
3'
MISCANTHUS
MISCANTHUS
HEMEROCALLIS SP.
BUDDLEIA
YUCCA FILAMENTOSA 2'
BETULA 10'
NIGRA
RHUS LANCINIATA
LONICERA SP.
ARBORVITAE
8'
euonymus
trans.
CORNUS ELEGANTISSIMA
TAXUS
TRANS.
TAXUS
TRANS
bluestone
BETULA NIGRA 8'
hedera
SALIX REPENS
SALIX
CAPREA
TAXUS TRANSPLANT
HYDRANGEA
QUERCIFOLIA
CORNUS BAILEYI

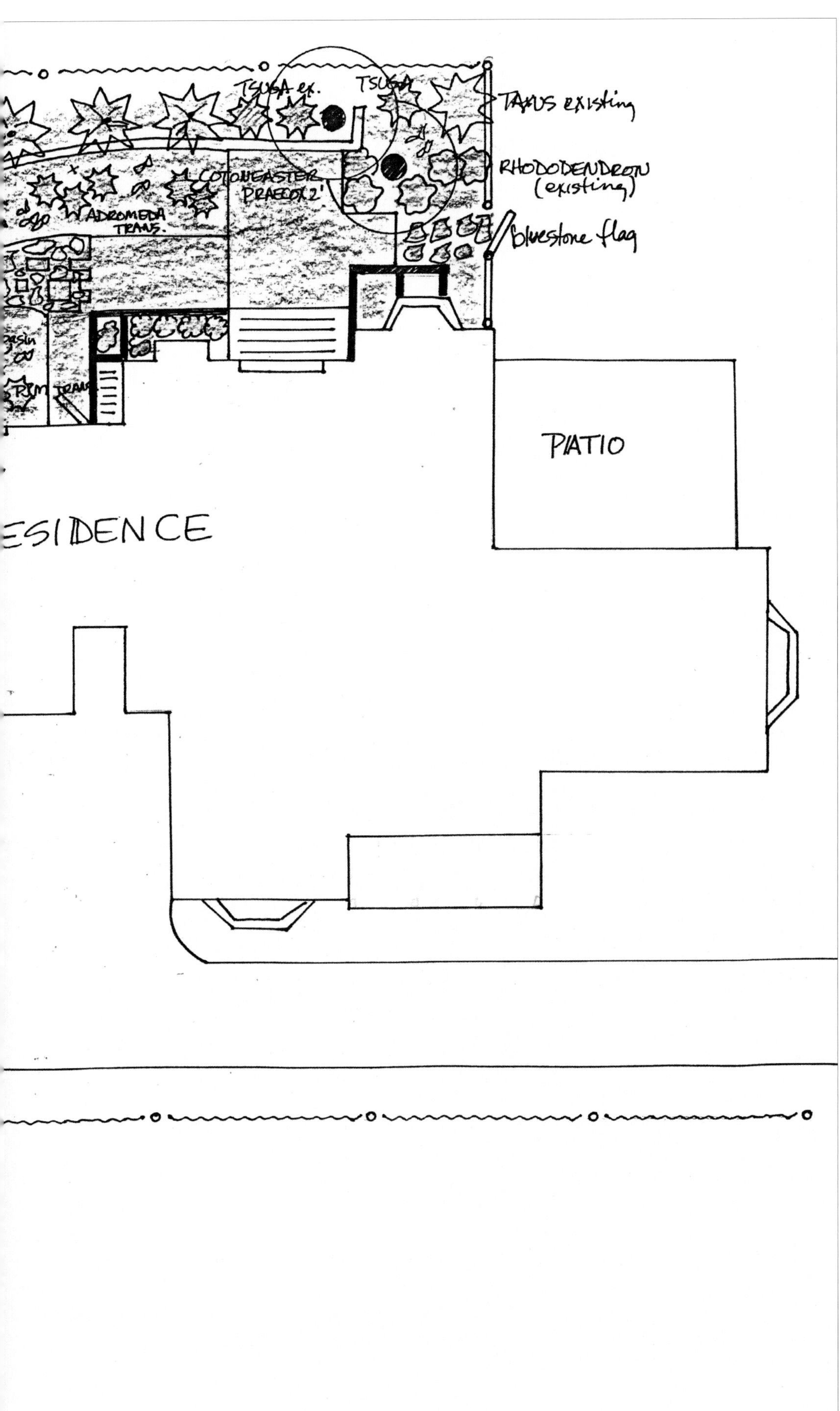

Left: Landscape design for the pool and patio. *Overleaf:* Nostalgic for the beauty of spring in New England, we created a little piece of the East Coast in this Midwestern woodland garden.

Top left: A more casual gravel surface replaced the pool terrace to aid in water management and sustain the old and new plant collections. ***Bottom left:*** A fall foliage moment contrasts with a panel of lawn instead of a covered pool for winter.

Right: Covered gate entry with emergent *Aruncus dioicus* leads to back garden. ***Overleaf:*** The perennial garden in early summer with the majesty of *Digitalis purpurea 'Camelot Rose'* and the first flush of shrub roses.

Farther Afield

The best way to learn about a place is to grow plants in it. Over the years, we've had the pleasure of working on gardens far from our base in the Midwest, and we have relished every opportunity to experiment in new zones, from seaside winds to desert heat. We're skilled at adapting and changing our usual approaches to design and implementation to the actual demands of the project.

These are often projects for clients with whom we are already working. Having the trust of our clients after development of their landscape has revealed new project challenges in different climes. Sometimes it's a move, more often the purchase of a second home. As trusted members of their "home team" we do the research needed at local public gardens, nurseries, garden centers, and neighboring properties to create the palette of plants. We then interview, select, and collaborate with local contractors and craftspeople to translate our design intentions into reality.

The bed layout within the wooden framework provides formality while the plantings extend the soft textures of the natural landscape.

Desert Oasis

Craig and Paul found the simple architecture of this modest townhouse community in the Catalina foothills a perfect foil for highlighting sculptural cactus and desert plants. They also didn't want to obstruct the magnificent views in any way. Tree yuccas, potted plants, found art, and natural pieces of wood and stone established an Arizonian palette. The team learned great respect for those who lived in this desert before modern conveniences were invented, and for the plants that had evolved adaptations to cope as well.

Opposite, top: Carved stone Conquistador fragment amid *Agave punctata*.
Opposite, bottom: Mesquite log planted with *Astrophytum myriostigma*.

Above: Walled patio with native *Yucca brevifolia* and *Carnegiea gigantea*.

Winter Haven

The small Palm Springs neighborhood of Winter Haven was all the rage for snowbirds in the 1960s. The simplicity and neutrality of this house allowed for extravagant planting selections like Bismarck palm, *Yucca rostrata*, brilliant bougainvillea, and all sorts of architectural cacti. Always the collector, Craig amassed vintage Gainey pottery and Willy Guhl containers to create growing space that would extend the garden onto patios and under the shelter of broad overhangs. This is where we learned the phrase "the most important palm trees in Palm Springs are your neighbor's" for the first time. The borrowed view of distant palms provides a layer of depth to the vistas and contrast with the wonderful cloud formations.

Above: Strong vertical elements and mounded forms create a sculpture garden of plants.

Top: Tequilla agaves provide bold contrast in color and form to the Green Ficus hedge.

Bottom: Domes of desert bromeliad fill a bowl planter covered with creeping ice plant.

Top: Stone slabs of various shapes but the same thickness offer a graceful ascent to the front entry.

Bottom: The distinctive natural wave patterns in the stone reflect the geological event of encasing an ancient beach millions of years ago.

House on the Hill

The appropriately named Wildwood community in southwest Michigan is a host to many wooded acres that share common wetlands and private beach access. This wonderful 1920s stucco cottage, named PenYBryn, is eighty-five steps up from the road, on the top of a sand dune and a six-plus acre lot. Deer, fox, squirrels, and myriad migrant and resident birds are the closest neighbors.

After visiting, James and Craig fell in love with this area of woods and water and started looking for a nearby lot for a future home. A few months later a friend called to asked if they would like to buy her place outright. They agreed immediately. The images shown here are the culmination of fifteen years of work by James, Paul, and Craig.

James and Craig replaced the gravel driveway with century-old street pavers as wheel tracks to create traction in the winter—except for the times of deepest snowfall. Large regional stone slabs were selected to replace the walkway. This was a feat; contractor friend Gunnar Piotter had to use a telescopic crane to guide them into place. They also removed all signs of cultivation from the planting space around the house and started a collection of faux-bois outdoor furniture and planters that seemed to fit right into the woods. A much-needed shed built by carpenter friend Bob Walker and salvaged from a flower show garden, was re-erected at the top of the drive.

This garden is magic in the spring with native hemlock, serviceberries, witch hazels, maple-leaf viburnum, leatherwood ferns, *hepatica*, and trilliums galore, all under the canopy of a climax dune woodland canopy of beech and oaks. We added both *Corylopsis* and easy-to-grow rhododendrons of all types that thrive in the acidic soil—plants we struggle with in one-zone-colder Illinois.

Above: Reclaimed street pavers in the driveway ensure passage in all weather.

Tropical Retreat

When friends and clients from Lake Forest decided to retire in the Riomar neighborhood of Vero Beach, Florida, they called us. The neighborhood streets are shaded by ancient live oak trees with resurrection fern and Spanish moss growing in the branches—a plant geek's paradise! The house itself was a nondescript midcentury ranch with an asphalt circle drive. It was ripe for Steve, the architect homeowner, to renovate. His wife, Susan, insisted that to live in Florida in retirement, she would require a sizable garden to call her own; she was the real catalyst for our involvement. Since we had a preexisting relationship that had built trust, the planning journey was easy and gratifying.

A location just two blocks from the beach meant bringing the structure up to hurricane code. Steve created a lanai for indoor/outdoor living and refreshed the stucco walls with a crisp white facelift, making a perfect backdrop to plants. We decided to remove the circular drive, which opened up much more space for tropical plants that in turn screen the house from the road. Extending the stucco to cover a garden wall and opening a gate in it also helped to focus attention on the landscape beyond. The tropical understory of the huge live oaks is amplified with elephant ears, ferns, fan palms, crinum lilies, *Clerodendrum*, and a specimen *Dombeya*.

A mature stand of bananas original to the landscape still lives proudly at the far end of the garden; we added a single new Bismarck palm for sculptural effect, and it's since become Susan's favorite plant. Brilliant shocks of hot pink bougainvillea and hibiscus create an almost jungle foliage effect with mixed palms and elephant ears. A distant bromeliad garden lolls under the shade of a mature stand of white bird of paradise that Susan is constantly tending and perfecting. This sleek white quartet of gardenias popping out amid the thousands of tropical textures provides an appealing memory of the white-and-green gardens of home for this Midwestern couple as they luxuriate here in the winter months.

Above: Ancient live oaks contrast with the low-slung white architecture.

Top: A bubbling fountain jar set within a quartet of gardenias offers a soothing sound for the lanai.

Bottom: The jungle character of the banana colony supports the strong geometry of the *Bismarkia nobilis*.

Old Shore Vineyard

Clients and friends from Chicago found a perfect getaway in Buchanan, Michigan: a twenty-acre parcel including a barn and an existing windbreak wall of native trees and a few old white pines. The owner, who has a degree in engineering and architecture, designed and supervised the construction of the agrarian-styled group of country house buildings. Once they discovered the sandy rolling hills were suited to growing wine grapes, a vineyard was born.

Old lichen-covered stone was perfect for a retaining wall that provides the visual foundation for this house on a rise while concealing the gravel drive from interior views. A small clapboard outbuilding set at the end of the new wall helps link the detached garage to the other buildings in view.

The challenges of wind exposure and the knowledge that the garden could receive only occasional maintenance helped guide us in the plant selections; often the choice was to use as close to straight species as possible for durability and hardiness. Lavender and thyme can thrive in these conditions as well as in intense sun, helped a bit by year-round good drainage in sandy soil.

This handy Canadian-born man and his incredibly active and hard-working American wife are a new version of the *American Gothic* couple; here they can celebrate the best the Midwest has to offer.

Opposite top: A found-timber arbor frames views within and beyond the enclosure. ***Opposite bottom:*** Organic stone planters display hardy succulents with iron gears interspersed, all to reference the simple, practical forms of an agrarian sensibility.

Above: A new stone wall and rugosa roses provide a visual ha-ha for the entry view to the farmhouse.

An Architectural Reclamation

Gardens at 900

Opposite: Plantings in the Blue, Yellow, and White Garden: rhubarb foliage, *Salvia* 'Blue Hill', and the yellow Cassia with Alliums.

Bottom: Visitor Guide rendering.

In 2010 Paul Klug and Craig decided it was time to create a home—for themselves as well as the business. One wintery Sunday morning while they were living in a condo in the Gold Coast neighborhood of Chicago, Paul announced: "A small David Adler hit the market!" A tiny real estate ad showing two gate houses and motor house piqued interest. Located in the northern suburb of Lake Forest, the property was the opposite of city living, but they were ready for a change. After a tour in heavy snow—which hid faulty roofs and concealed problematic soils—they made an offer that was accepted in just a week. Fifteen years later and after a major renovation, it serves as a personal and a professional base.

The 2.68-acre property was formerly part of the 150-acre Elawa Farm—an anagram for the owners, Elsa and A. Watson Armour. The three buildings offered for sale were a gracious entry to what was a gentleman's farm, akin to those found in England. Interestingly, the main house was never built, but Adler was asked to refine and convert structures intended as staff quarters into a private retreat for the Armour family. Craig and Paul are only the fourth owners since 1917. They named the property "The Gardens at 900," in reference to its original address, 900 North Telegraph Road. The rest of the acreage is now owned and managed in combination by the city and a private not-for-profit foundation. The farm complex hosts demonstration programs for healthy living, based on organic practices for the garden and home.

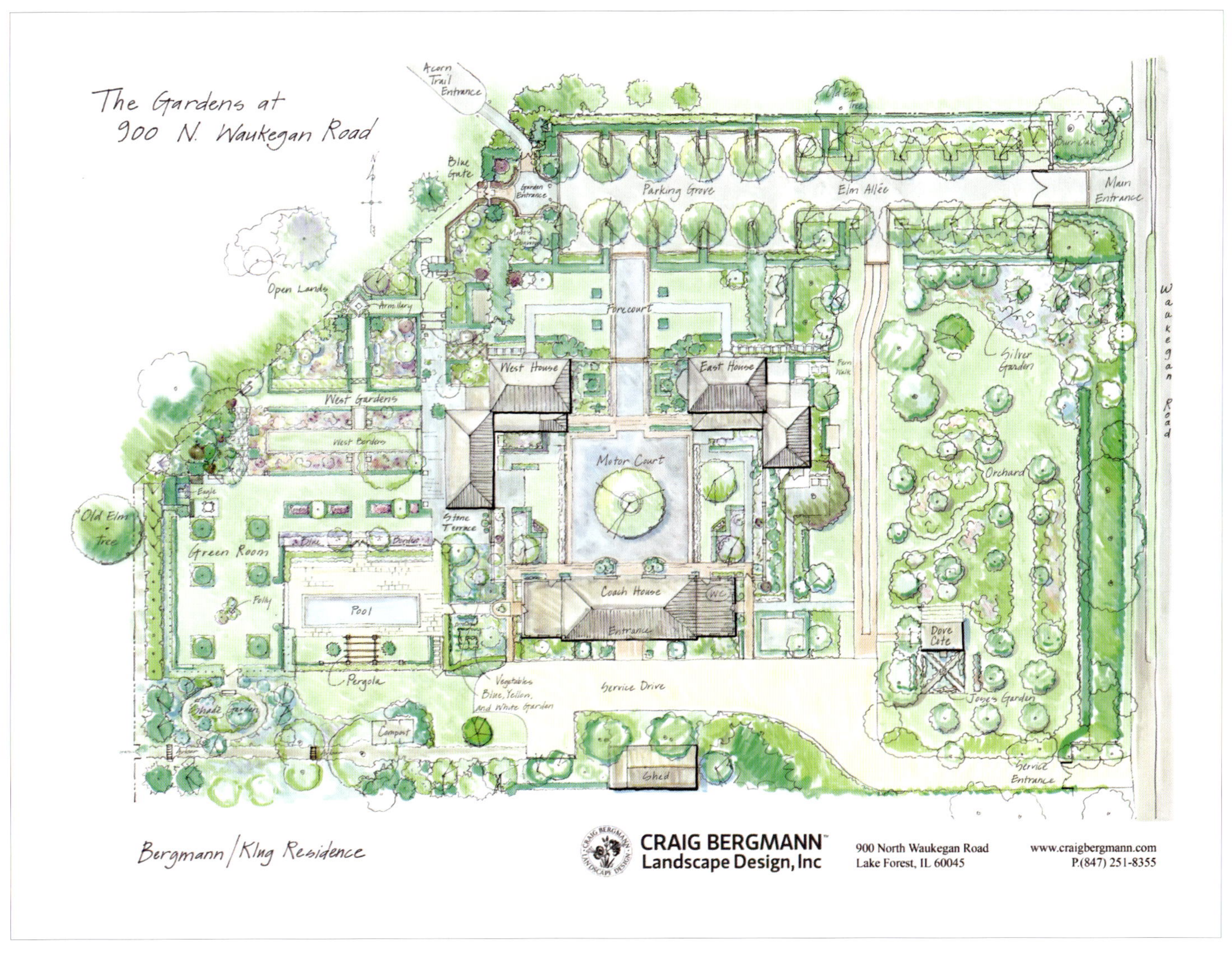

Above: View from the Blue Border to the rose parterres, 2012.

Opposite: Morning view of the ribbon driveway through the turf of the orchard and a lone staddle stone.

Overleaf: July in the West Borders.

Paul and Craig were enticed by the opportunity to save a derelict but gemlike property—and excited enough to not even test soils before buying the place. Ralph Rodney Root had designed plantings for the Armours in the early 1920s, but few remnants to hint at his original intent remained. American elms that could be seen in historical photographs were gone, replaced by meager-in-comparison Norway maples. Old yew hedges had been tortured by constant deer browsing, but invasive burning bush and barberry were thriving. Much to the couple's surprise their first April, old varieties of peonies and German irises randomly emerged with a fortified daffodil, crocus, and tulip here and there. Each of these perennial survivors has been treasured and, when possible, propagated. They decided early on to share propagated plants with friends, clients, and visitors to the gardens for free. These old-fashioned Elawa Farm flowers abound now all over the country, their varieties destined to live on.

The first plants for the new Gardens at 900 were transplanted from The Country Garden, the former nursery and garden center which had been sold to fund this new project and nursery location. We disassembled the plant collections from our various display gardens and moved them and our vital old rose propagation stock. The boxwood hedges that back the main herbaceous borders were the remnants of a holiday market sale the previous Christmas season.

We've created ten distinct display gardens here: the Entry Allée; the Motor Court; the Orchard; the Harvest Garden (if you help pick, you can keep some of the produce); the Herbaceous Borders; the Blue Border (in homage to Paul as it's his favorite color, and the color of the complex's 144 shutters!); the Pool Garden; the Blue, Yellow and White Garden; the Green Room;

Opposite: The Folly with a stone capital and a column framed by the Shade Garden entry arch of *Fagus sylvatica* 'Purple Fountain'.

Above: The West Borders frame a view of the West House.

Overleaf: The West Gardens.

and the Shade Garden. Our primary purpose was to create an interesting journey through various themed spaces. We blurred the property boundaries and borrowed views to keep visitors guessing just how big the actual space is, what is around every bend.

To best complement the Federal revival architectural style, we leaned into history and scale, barring any plants or materials that were exotic, invasive, or just "too new" to blend with the setting. This subjective approach still allows for plenty of aesthetic license, however. We've included a few tropical beauties in pots to highlight interesting plants available today—after all, the gardens are a showroom for clients and the public and a laboratory for staff.

Architectural salvage, repositioned plants, repurposed building materials, found objects and furniture—from this site and others —add a patina to these relatively new gardens. Nothing is to too perfect, too clean, too arranged. We create so many formal estate landscapes that it's a pleasure to present a more casual lifestyle here and, in our way, honor the original intent of the compound as an area for workers, albeit a pretty one. Today one gate house is our home; Paul's interior design office and showroom occupies the larger gate house; and Craig's design studio fills the motor/coach house.

Above: Outside Craig's office door is a granite cobblestone path bordered by *Euphorbia cyparissias* 'Fen's Ruby'.

Opposite: Cast-stone Pan fountain, original to the property, with a weeping Japanese maple.

Overleaf: Greenhouse container plant collection in summer with *Brugmansia suaveolans* in full trumpet.

A resident Norwich terrier pack of four are on the payroll as the first line of defense against an overpopulation of chipmunks, mice, and rabbits, although winter mole and vole activities seem to elude them. It's hilarious to see a terrier rump disappear into a box hedge and then watch a head pop out twenty feet down the line—they're not large enough to do serious damage. With no chemical intervention for wildlife control, we are sure that all creatures great and small that visit here go away happier and probably a bit plumper. "We grow and harvest enough for all" is the mantra. Remember that a big garden will attract nature in all its manifestations.

Keeping the garden tidy enough for frequent visitors' eyes has meant scaling back ideas about presentation. Russ and Craig have adopted the standard line for folks touring: "If you see a weed, pull it if you dare!" This garden will never be finished, perfect, big enough, or easy to take care of, but it feels like a true home, and we hope all who visit pick up on its welcoming hospitality and warmth.

Above: The edge of the Shade Garden.

Top: Cherry, Craig, and Paul in the Blue, Yellow, and White Garden. ***Bottom:*** Coach House facade with potted myrtle topiary and clipped box and yews.

Above: Spring in the orchard with old and new fruit trees, old roses, and naturalizing spring bulbs.

Above: Gravel-jointed bluestone stone path behind the West Borders.
Overleaf: The Shade Garden with emergent azaleas and woodland ephemerals.

Above: Watson and Pepper in the spring Blue, Yellow, and White Garden.
Opposite, top: Snow whispers over the forms of the garden in winter.

Opposite, bottom: Early twentieth-century English faux-bois bench against an impressive backdrop of *Petasites japonica*.

Dedication

Spring flower collage by Stephanie Lindemann.

On our life journeys, we have lost two integral members of the CBLD family. James Grigsby, Craig's former life partner and the cofounder of CBLD in 1981, and Deanna Buvala, Russell's wife and our senior propagator at the CBLD nursery in 2023. Both of these dear people carried two of the original torches lighting the way through the uncharted territory of growing a horticultural business. From them, the seeds sown have not only germinated, but matured into the successful company it is today. We will be forever grateful for their love and strength.

To Paul, my love and my biggest cheerleader and defender. If I say I am going to do something, he just accepts that it will happen. I am a very lucky person to have his unlimited belief in me and my abilities. To my parents, who were always my support system through life's challenges. Their love, teachings, and mentoring shaped me to know how to care for others. Their nurturing taught me to appreciate and treasure all living things, even if I didn't like them all. So here's to opossums and bindweed!

To Russ, my friend and my constant support at CBLD. If I say we need to do something, he gets it done with enthusiasm and wisdom, and knows how to make things best, and how to handle me! I am humbled to have been able to work with someone of his talent, unparalleled in nuance and excellence, and to have shared this voyage together for these decades.

—Craig Bergmann

I have benefitted from the support of many people who complete me, and I dedicate this book to them. My parents' unwavering connection with me throughout my life has been remarkably sustaining. To the professors at the University of Illinois, especially Dianne Noland and Dr. Marvin Carbonneau, who generously gave me my beginnings in horticulture. I met my wife, Deanna, who was my light for thirty-seven years, in Dianne's herbaceous perennial class, and we had a wonderful life together. She was always known to be a quiet person, and now it seems I am speechless. Simply put, we were symbiotic. She is missed every day by everyone who knew her. To our two sons, Alexander and Matthew: I am very proud of you. You personify everything that I believe in. And of course, to Craig, about whom I cannot speak more highly as a leader, person, and friend. He is one of the best people I have had the honor to know. And just recently, I have had the unbelievable fortune to have met yet another person who enriches my life and work, and I would not been able to work on this book without her support. Samantha Peckham is an unbelievable horticulturalist and is an extremely supportive individual. It is a privilege to have been so supported by so many. When people feed your soul, you can truly shine.

—Russell Buvala

Acknowledgments

Spring companioning at its finest in a friend's garden.

The many talented members of CBLD, past and present—our landscape architects, designers, gardeners, horticulturalists, technicians, and support staff—are the reason for our success. Without them, we would never have been able to produce the projects highlighted in this book. The current management team of Dawn Monfardini, John Palenske, Kenon Boehm, Russell Buvala, Nora Kennedy, Keith Carlsen, and Holly Siebeck is helping to carry the company toward a bright and stable future, making us stronger and better. A special thank you to Holly for her expertise in coordinating the materials for this project. Every day, we are humbled by everyone's dedication.

To Donald Mathieson, our friend and skilled landscape project manager during the birthing years of the Gardens at 900. His dedication to installing all the plant materials transplanted from the Country Garden helped to keep things alive and provided the focus for getting all established. Most importantly, our trust in Donny to manage this gargantuan task allowed all of us to keep working on our client jobs at the same time. The maturity of the wonderful garden spaces now is a tribute to his success with us in the beginning.

Over the decades, numerous artisans and contractors have helped realize the work we have designed but could never have installed ourselves. A special thanks to Masonry by Fernando Inc., Advanced Sprinkler Systems Inc., Buss Landscape Company, Boilini Company, Design Alternatives, Artisan Woodworks Ltd., Doulas & Company, and Norbert Pabuda of Norton Inc. There are too many nursery and materials suppliers to name here, but to all who have worked with us and provided wonderful products to fulfill the plant lists and hardscapes of our designs, thank you.

A special shout-out to our friend Roy Diblik for his gracious foreword as well as friendship, wisdom, and his ability to always plant the seed of horticulture in folks in a way that ensures it will continue to work in the service of our earth's health.

Thanks are certainly due to the multiple photographers whose work is featured here, especially Scott Shigley for his always-ready support, Donald Bolak, Lynda Oyama Bryan, and Judith Bromley, who have also graced these pages with their art.

Thank you to The Monacelli Press for their steadfast commitment to our first-time effort. The guidance and professionalism of Elizabeth White, editor-at-large, has been pivotal to the process. To Stacee Gravelle Lawrence, for her talent and enthusiasm making the process painless of editing our often run-on thoughts, and to Jena Sher, whose elegant design has brought our work to life on the page.

Lastly, special thanks to our clients, who allow us to share their private worlds and homes and trust us to create their dream landscapes.

First published in the United States by The Monacelli Press.

Library of Congress Control Number: 2024926922
ISBN: 978158093 691 0

Photographs by Scott Shigley
except as noted below:
Craig Bergmann 2, 4, 15 top, 18, 19, 24–25, 64–65, 82, 94, 106 below left, 108, 144, 186, 262
Donald Bolak 212, 216–17, 218, 219, 220–21, 257 top
Judith Bromley 9, 15 below, 128, 132, 133
Linda Oyama Bryan 8, 11, 26, 28, 30, 31, 34–35, 36, 37, 48, 54–55, 60, 61, 62, 63, 66, 78, 96, 97, 100, 101, 102, 103, 106 top, 106 below right, 114, 136, 138–39, 140, 141,142–43, 166, 168 ,170–71, 173, 174, 175, 188–89, 190
Deana Buvala 23
Stephanie Lindemann 14, 258

Design: Jena Sher Graphic Design

Printed in China

Monacelli
A Phaidon Company
111 Broadway
New York, New York 10006
www.phaidon.com/monacelli